Victorian Britain

VICTORIAN BRITAIN

MICHAEL JENNER

WEIDENFELD & NICOLSON
LONDON

First published in Great Britain in 1999
By Weidenfeld & Nicolson

This edition printed 2003 for Eagle Editions Ltd, 11 Heathfield, Royston, Herts SG8 5BW, UK

A CIP catalogue record for this book is available from the British Library
ISBN 0 297 82514 3

Designed by Harry Green
Edited by Jonathan Hilton
Set in Century Expanded
Printed in Italy

Weidenfeld & Nicolson
The Orion Publishing Group Ltd
5 Upper St Martin's Lane
London WC2H 9EA

PHOTOGRAPHS
(Page 1)
The Scott Monument, built in 1844, is a striking Gothic landmark
on the Edinburgh skyline.

(Page 2)
Queen Victoria surveys the scene at Windsor Castle,
one of her favourite residences.

CONTENTS

INTRODUCTION

—◆—

Current perceptions of the Victorian age are tinged with an aura of sepia-tinted antiquity. Most personal portraits of the era are remote and formal, with a preponderance of stiff-necked males glowering at the camera through forbiddingly biblical beards, making it difficult for us to imagine the Victorians as ever having been young or full of fun. Then there is the grim background picture, familiar from Dickens, of a grinding social reality of poverty and misery, with wealth built on exploitation. But this is only one side of the coin. In many ways, the Victorian age must have been every bit as exciting and colourful as our own. There were constant technological innovations affecting every aspect of life, which all contributed to a heady climate of ceaseless change.

This book is concerned mainly with the physical legacy that the Victorians left behind. There is a breathtaking array of artefacts and architecture to help us recapture the essence of the period, from country houses and railway stations to seaside piers and civic buildings. The Victorians seem endowed with boundless energy and an indomitable purpose, which we tend to see as supreme self-confidence. Yet it is possible to interpret their brasher productions as brave attempts to paper over doubts about where they and their world were heading. For this was an age that often hid its fears and confusions behind boldly expressed convictions.

If one were to take a single symbol to express the genius of the age, it has to be the Great Exhibition of 1851. Not only did it bring together all the manufacturing, technical and design skills of the day, it was also the country's first large-scale event aimed at informing and entertaining the general public. The Victorians built their glittering Crystal Palace not as an end in itself, but because they needed such a showcase to contain the wealth of their exhibits.

Anybody born in the first half of the twentieth century has grown up in the shadow of Victorian achievements, and it has been a hard act to follow. But now with the dawn of the millennium, as our Victorian ancestors slip gracefully away into the deeper recesses of history, so it is possible for us to view them and their world with greater clarity.

SPIRITS OF THE AGE

Down House in the village of Downe, Kent, was home to the scientist Charles Darwin from 1842 to 1882.

A modest house at 24 Cheyne Row in an ordinary Georgian terrace in Chelsea is as good a place as any to begin this whirlwind exploration of the Victorian era, since from 1834 until his death in 1881, it was the home of Thomas Carlyle, eminent writer and historian. Apart from its celebrity association, Carlyle's house also illustrates the fact that the Victorians inherited a Georgian environment that they found rather lacking in interest. For the Carlyles, in line with the new Victorian taste for gloomy interiors, covered the light pine panelling of their Georgian house with paper stained dark to resemble oak.

In this age of big issues, with serious thinkers delivering prophet-like judgements from their individual mounds of moral high ground, Carlyle was the sage of sages. He had something to say about everything, and all the crosscurrents of nineteenth-century thought swirled and eddied through his drawing room. Dismissive of personal happiness as an end in itself, Carlyle proposed views, including the notion that imminent social chaos could only be avoided by accepting the leadership of men of exceptional quality, which now sound dangerously totalitarian. But Carlyle was not alone in devising extreme solutions for society's ills.

Another Georgian house was home from 1842 until 1882 to a far less assertive man, but one whose ideas were to have greater effect. During his residence at Down House in Kent, Charles Darwin worked up his theories on evolution and wrote *The Origin of Species* and *The Descent of Man*. The shocking notion that human beings, then generally believed to be formed literally in God's own image, were actually descended through apes and monkeys was social and religious dynamite. Darwin's theories sparked off the most heated and impassioned controversy of the century with its revolutionary challenge to the biblical *Book of Genesis*. The Bishop of Oxford did his best to ridicule Darwin. The humble scientist was denounced as the most dangerous man in the country.

Karl Marx, the man who really did fit that description, dispatched a dedicated copy of his subversive book *Das Kapital* to Darwin. Marx and his German compatriot, Engels, hardly qualify to most observers as great Victorians, but the fact remains that the body of their analytical work, which was to have such devastating consequences for the entire world in the twentieth century, was produced in nineteenth-century England. William Morris, now remembered chiefly as a cuddly idealist with a talent for designing medievalist wallpaper and textiles, accepted Marxist theory virtually *in toto*. Yet what drove Morris to his own brand of socialism was a profound hatred of modern civilization:

> Forget six counties overhung with smoke,
> Forget the snorting steam and piston stroke,
> Forget the spreading of the hideous town;
> Think rather of the pack-horse on the down,
> And dream of London, small and white and clean,
> The clear Thames bordered by its gardens green.

Morris's favourite retreat was the Tudor manor of Kelmscott situated by the Thames in Oxfordshire. He described the ancient manor house almost as if it were a person: '. . . it has a sadness about it which is not gloom but the melancholy born of beauty,' a wistful quality that he found 'very stimulating to the imagination'. This was where Morris drew strength and inspiration, both for his art and his lifelong campaign against the shoddy materialism of his times. In this, he shared much with John Ruskin, who retreated to Brantwood on Coniston Water, overlooking one of the finest natural prospects in the Lake District.

Most Victorian art was a flight from the present. The Pre-Raphaelites, who owed much to Ruskin's critical support, were deeply imbued with the spirit of the past, whether it was medieval England or Renaissance Italy. *Gentle Music of Bygone Days* by Roddam Spencer Stanhope and *Love Among the Ruins* by Edward Burne-Jones, just two of many paintings on display at Wightwick Manor, say it all in their nostalgic titles alone. Social reality gets hardly a look in. When the artist George Frederic Watts returned to London from a tour of Italy, he was so shocked by what he saw that he painted *Found Drowned* and *Under a Dry Arch*. These harsh images of human suffering stand out among the rest of his idealized symbolic work in the Watts Gallery at Compton in Surrey, a building that was commissioned by the artist shortly before his death.

Although this was in so many ways a progressive age, with new manufacturing processes and inventions such as the railway and the telephone, when it came to art and architecture,

Karl Marx found his final resting-place in 1883 in north London's Highgate Cemetery, but his ideas went marching on.

WORKERS OF ALL LANDS
UNITE

Tower Bridge, maritime gateway to London, is a typically Victorian blend of new engineering and old architecture.

the Victorian response was invariably historicism. Ford Madox Brown's series of murals in Manchester Town Hall stop well short of celebrating the very industry that had created the Manchester miracle in the first place. Like its counterpart, Rochdale Town Hall, the building is unashamedly Gothic in style. Similarly, London's famous Tower Bridge, a proud symbol of contemporary commerce, hid its technology under a cloak of medieval design. Even an inconsequential electricity sub-station built in 1895 in Cheltenham might disguise itself as a miniature copy of the Palazzo Strozzi in Florence. As the famous Victorian architect Norman Shaw reflected: 'When you come to think of it, what are any of us doing but copying the styles of the past?'

Mobility was another major element of the Victorian period, with a broad spectrum of people travelling all over the country and even abroad for the first time. Rural communities were sucked into the towns and cities. But this flurry of movement contrasts with the underlying desire of the public for a kind of stability, such as that represented by Victoria and Albert shining like fixed stars in an eternal firmament above a society in turmoil. The royal couple came to symbolize the timeless virtues of duty, tradition and family in a world riding a roller-coaster of change.

Victoria's grief at Albert's death in 1861 cast a shadow of bereavement over the remainder of the nineteenth century, giving us today a sense of sobriety that we still think of as being quintessentially Victorian. *Gravitas* was very much the order of the day, as befitted the world's mightiest colonial power. A large mural in the Foreign and Commonwealth Office shows an awesome *Britannica Pacificatrix* assuming God-like powers and responsibilities over her subject peoples: 'To the motherland they offer aid and council. Friends acclaim the righteous peace.' Just in case the message was not already clear enough, there are also some judicious quotes from the Old Testament: '. . . for thou shalt judge the folk righteously and govern the nations upon the earth.'

The Victorians do indeed appear to have had a grand vision of themselves and of their achievements, and they celebrated the great men of their age, or, rarely, a great woman such as Florence Nightingale, with heroic statues and monuments. Our towns, cities, parks and gardens are full of them. Everywhere we look, we can still see images of these colossi who once trod the earth in their seven-league boots. Whether cast in bronze or carved in marble, our Victorian ancestors seem endowed with a naturally statuesque quality, which also forms an essential and intriguing part of their enduring appeal.

VICTORIA AND ALBERT

The statues of Victoria in Birmingham and of Albert in Liverpool are typical of the many erected to the royal couple throughout Britain in the course of the nineteenth century. It is partly due to such likenesses of Victoria in her later years that we tend to see her as the sour-faced, portly widow who became a grand matriarchal symbol for the entire nation. Albert, by contrast, who died at the tender age of forty-two, remains in the collective memory forever preserved in the full vigour of his manhood. It takes some effort of imagination to recall that the Victoria who acceded to the throne in 1837 was a romantic eighteen-year-old girl who fell head-over-heels in love with her Prince Charming. She found Albert 'excessively handsome' and noted 'such beautiful blue eyes, an exquisite nose, and such a pretty mouth, with delicate moustachios, and . . . a beautiful

figure, broad in the shoulders and a fine waist'. It took the British public a bit longer to appreciate the virtues of the Prince Consort. Behind the scenes, however, the German-born Albert turned out to have a very keen political understanding of Britain and he was instrumental in shaping the emerging constitutional monarchy. Albert soon proved invaluable to Victoria as an astute advisor. His practical services to the country were considerable, but his many achievements have been overshadowed by his spectacular success in launching the Great Exhibition of 1851. Real recognition of Albert's achievements, however, followed only after his death in 1861. The many places bearing his name, from the Royal Albert Hall to Albert Square – not forgetting the many pubs with 'Albert' in their name – convey some measure of his abiding memory.

GLADSTONE VS DISRAELI

Gladstone, sculpted in white marble in the Central Lobby of the Houses of Parliament, and Disraeli, modelled in bronze on the steps of St George's Hall, Liverpool, were two fiercely competitive political heavyweights. Victoria, like many of her subjects, did not warm to the Liberal prime minister William Ewart Gladstone, a stern High Church Anglican with Nonconformist tendencies, whom she once famously described as 'an old, wild, and incomprehensible man', who spoke to Her Majesty in private audience 'as if I were a public meeting'. Benjamin Disraeli, an advocate of Tory democracy, was an urbane Jew who found his spiritual home in the Church of England. He captivated the Queen with his easy charm, which may not have been entirely sincere to judge from his remark: 'Everyone likes flattery, and when it comes to royalty, you should lay it on with a trowel.' But Disraeli helped lure the grieving Victoria back into public life after Albert's death and he boosted her self-esteem by bestowing on her the grand title of Empress of India. After Disraeli's death in 1881, Victoria visited his country house of Hughenden in Buckinghamshire and spent some time on her own in his study in order to mourn the passing of a trusted and loyal friend. Gladstone's lasting memorial should have been Irish Home Rule, a cause for which he took huge political risks, but this initiative failed and, in 1886, resulted in the splitting of the Liberal Party.

MARX IN MANCHESTER

Karl Marx, a penniless refugee from Germany, while working on his book *Das Kapital*, published in 1867, was in frequent contact with his friend and sponsor Friedrich Engels, author of the equally subversive *Condition of the Working Class in England*. When Marx first visited Engels in Manchester in 1845, the two would meet in the secluded medieval alcove of Chetham's Library seen here. In a letter to Engels in 1870, Marx reminisced: 'During the last few days I have again spent a good deal of time sitting at the four-sided desk in the alcove where we sat together twenty four years ago. I am very fond of the place.' The actual desk, as described by Marx, is still there. It is not without some irony that the capitalist stronghold of nineteenth-century Manchester may thus be acclaimed as the cradle of communism.

MORRIS AT KELMSCOTT

The Elizabethan house of Kelmscott Manor, on the pastoral upper reaches of the Thames near Lechlade, occupied a special place in the life of William Morris for a quarter of a century, from 1871 until his death in 1896. He described the peculiar charm of this particular patch of English countryside as a haven from all the troubles and complexities of the outside world. But to Morris, Kelmscott was more than a refuge: 'As others love the race of man through their loves or children, so I love the earth through this small space of it.' It is still possible to share the Morris vision of this idyllic location, which seems mysteriously shielded from the ravages of the machine age against which Morris campaigned so vigorously in his art and writings.

PRE-RAPHAELITE VISIONS

The painting of 1857 *A Dream of the Past: Sir Isumbras at the Ford* by John Everett Millais is in the Lady Lever Art Gallery in Port Sunlight, and it encapsulates some of the essential features of Pre-Raphaelite art, with its medieval inspiration, mystic longings, bright colours and intricate detail. Notable collections of Pre-Raphaelite art are also to be found in the Walker Art Gallery, Liverpool; the Tate Gallery, London; the Barber Institute and Museum & Art Gallery, Birmingham. The works of Millais and his fellow Pre-Raphaelites William Holman Hunt, Dante Gabriel Rossetti and Edward Burne-Jones were, for a long time, regarded as run-of-the-mill Victoriana. Critical opinion now awards them their proper place in art history as noble expressions of Victorian nostalgic yearnings for an idealized, lost world of perfection.

THE WATTS GALLERY

George Frederic Watts (1817–1904) became one of the most acclaimed Victorian artists rather late in life. His individual concept of art as a means of expressing eternal truths was not properly appreciated until he was in his 70s. Unlike many of his successful contemporaries, Watts accorded fame and money very much a secondary role. He would paint for no fee or donate a work for charity. With increasing wealth, Watts could afford to keep anything he wanted for himself. In 1904, the year of his death, the resulting personal collection of paintings, drawings and sculpture was brought together in a purpose-built gallery at Compton, Surrey. The works on display range from allegorical canvases, with titles such as *Hope* or *Time*, to the towering plaster model for his statue of the poet Tennyson. Mainly featuring original works by the artist himself, the Watts Gallery is a unique time capsule of Victorian art.

HAWKER'S HUT

Perched up on the cliffs near Morwenstow in Cornwall is a tiny hut. Surely the National Trust's smallest property, this makeshift structure was cobbled together with bits of driftwood and ship's wreckage by the legendary Parson Hawker. Here, wearing an ordinary seaman's jersey and seaboots under his cassock, the cleric would smoke pipes of opium while he composed his poetry. Hawker was regularly confronted with the harsh realities of life and death. Among his more unenviable duties was the burying of drowned seafarers who were washed up on the rugged coast of his parish in north Cornwall. He would occasionally play practical jokes, such as disguising himself as a mermaid by lying on a rock covered in seaweed. Parson Hawker was a real Victorian eccentric who still enjoys a degree of notoriety in these parts.

HARDY'S COTTAGE

In 1840, Thomas Hardy was born in this humble cottage in Higher Bockhampton, Dorset. Hardy's novels, such as *Far from the Madding Crowd* of 1874 and *Tess of the D'Urbervilles* of 1891, are, on one level, an adieu to the pre-railway English countryside, as symbolized by his fictional Wessex. On a deeper level, Hardy portrays individual humans as powerless creatures pitted against eternal forces. In *Jude the Obscure* of 1895, Hardy moved into the dangerous territory of sexuality seen as an implacable natural power. Although Hardy was a true child of the Victorian era, he did challenge some of its bland assumptions, attracting much criticism in the process. But Hardy remains highly popular and one of the most enduring of the heavyweight Victorian novelists.

ONE FOOT IN THE PAST

Highclere Castle, Berkshire, was designed by Charles Barry, the architect of the Houses of Parliament.

A rising out of the Berkshire countryside like some rural version of the Houses of Parliament, Highclere Castle presents a noble aspect. The striking resemblance of Highclere to the architect Charles Barry's better-known work at the Palace of Westminster is hardly coincidental, since he was working on both projects at the end of the 1830s. Barry's heady mixture of Gothic and Classical styles struck a resonant chord in the Victorian soul. Benjamin Disraeli, on first seeing Highclere, declared: 'How scenical! How scenical!' In fact, Disraeli's later internal remodelling of his own country house, located at Hughenden in Buckinghamshire, betrays this same love of Gothic detail deployed purely as a pleasing decorative device.

The revival of the Middle Ages was the leitmotif in the design of country houses for the remainder of the nineteenth century. However, in keeping with the serious mood of the times, a high degree of authenticity was often demanded by the clients. When William Morris commissioned architect Philip Webb to design him a new home near the village of Upton in Kent, he asked for something 'very medieval in spirit'. The building known as the Red House, now in the London surburb of Bexleyheath, was the result, which was described by Dante Gabriel Rossetti, the English poet and painter, as 'more a poem than a house . . . but an admirable place to live in'. Still proving Rossetti's point, the Red House remains a splendid private residence, while standing for something special in English domestic architecture. Although it was obviously inspired by the medieval tradition, its simplicity marks it out as a decidedly fresh reinterpretation of the past.

The Red House witnessed the birth of the Arts and Crafts Movement in England, as well as launching Philip Webb on his architectural career. Although Webb built relatively little during his lifetime, he took enormous care over even the smallest intricacies of his houses and their internal arrangements. At Standen in Sussex, for example, one can see the full fruition of the Webb style in a country house he designed for the wealthy London-based solicitor James Beale. This luxury weekend retreat of 1892–4 is inspired more by the homely forms of local vernacular than any soaring visions of the Gothic past.

Old English domesticity is also apparent at Wightwick Manor near Wolverhampton, where the paint manufacturer Theodore Mander had his half-timbered house of 1887–93 fitted out with such advanced features as electric lighting, central heating and a Turkish bath. But no such modernity was allowed to pervade the decor, the Great Parlour being a replica of an Elizabethan great hall, complete with a minstrel gallery. A similar mix of state-of-the-art technology and medieval nostalgia lies at the heart of William Armstrong's rural abode in Northumberland. Designed by Norman Shaw, Cragside achieves a stunning effect – more than a match for the rugged splendour of its natural setting. Armstrong had made his fortune on Tyneside manufacturing arms, and his country house was grand enough to be used for entertaining the likes of the Prince of Wales in 1884, which showed how the new industrial aristocracy was making its mark on society. Armstrong's Cragside pioneered the use of light bulbs and water-generated electricity.

Norman Shaw's favoured brand of Queen Anne retro was more often applied to smaller houses, such as the romantic Old Swan House of 1875, which was built on the Chelsea Embankment in London. Even in the bustling modernity of this huge metropolis, dreams of the past continued to influence the way people lived. At number 18 Stafford Terrace, a typical Kensington townhouse where the illustrator Linley Sambourne took up residence in the 1870s, some of the windows contain stained glass of a distinctly medieval feel. Not far away from here, at Leighton House, it is still possible to admire Victorian nostalgia at its most exotic in the Arab Hall, with its spirited attempt to reproduce an Islamic interior using authentic materials.

Arguably the most extravagant indulgence in nostalgic architecture, whether oriental or medieval, is to the credit of the 3rd Marquis of Bute. Fuelled by a massive fortune, which reputedly made him the wealthiest man in the country, Bute engaged William Burges to supervise from 1868 the remodelling of Cardiff Castle. Burges followed this in 1875 with the construction of a fairytale castle in the wooded hills outside Cardiff. Castell Coch, perfectly preserved since its completion more than a hundred years ago, sums up the essence of a rich Victorian's fairytale version of the Middle Ages.

Meanwhile, William Leigh's brave attempt at Woodchester Park Mansion, in the remote depths of Gloucestershire, to re-create a more dutiful replica of the medieval past, was

The Red House, built at Bexleyheath, was designed by Philip Webb for William Morris as a Victorian interpretation of medieval architecture.

Knightshayes Court, Devon, is a Victorian Gothic country house designed by William Burges.

ultimately left unfinished, having financially ruined its owner in the process. Arundel Castle contains one of the most compelling examples of Victorian medievalism within the shell of a genuine medieval building. And for good measure, the Duke of Norfolk also built a church nearby that was closely modelled on the chapel of Mont St Michel in Normandy, which has in the end found its true destiny as Arundel's Roman Catholic Cathedral.

Nineteenth-century nostalgia did not always confine itself to the Middle Ages when seeking a reference point. For its showy exteriors, Waddesdon Manor in Buckinghamshire, built between 1874 and 1879, takes its inspiration directly from Renaissance France. The Manor's wealthy owner, Baron Ferdinand de Rothschild, clearly wanted nothing but the real thing, for he instructed his French architect to design something that would convincingly pass muster among the châteaux of the Loire. Even more exotic in style, the oriental *tour de force* of the Arab Hall, which is set in the baronial setting of Cardiff Castle, shows the extent to which Victorian patrons would experiment with any style from the past that happened to take their fancy.

It was only with the dawning of the twentieth century that Victorian nostalgia reluctantly let go its hold and began to give way to something more contemporary in style. But even an acclaimed 'modern' architect such as Charles Rennie Mackintosh made little impact with his revolutionary Hill House at Helensburgh of 1902, while the nineteenth-century love affair with the Middle Ages endured even as late as 1910, as we can see with Edwin Lutyens at the Norman Revival Castle Drogo in Devon.

In the same way as their Victorian predecessors, the Edwardians were perfectly happy with mock-baronial, while showing a marked leaning towards the Baroque, as in the work carried out between 1904 and 1907 at Oldway in Paignton, Devon, for Mr Paris Eugene Singer. This scion of the sewing machine dynasty modelled his amazing alterations on the Palace of Versailles. He even arranged for scaffolding to be erected in the Galerie des Glaces at Versailles just so that his painter, Lebrun, could study the ceiling in detail and obtain exactly the right colours. Such was the hubris of those times that this was considered par for the course. In a curious change of fortunes, Paignton Council purchased Oldway in 1946 and converted it for use as a civic centre.

STANDEN

Philip Webb, a lifelong friend of William Morris, built this country house in West Sussex between 1892 and 1894 for the wealthy solicitor James Beale. Webb, at this late stage in his career, could pick and choose his clients, preferring the select few who were acquainted with the style of his work and 'able to judge of what would be the finished effect of that which I should agree to carry out'. Happily, Webb and Beale enjoyed a perfect understanding. The result at Standen is one of the purest expressions of Webb's Vernacular Revival, which draws its inspiration from traditional motifs, such as picturesque chimneystacks, pitched roofs and tile-hung façades. Pale imitations of Webb's distinctive style are popular with the architects of today's superstores.

WIGHTWICK MANOR

This country house of 1887–93, just outside Wolverhampton, is a late-Victorian design by Edward Ould, a specialist in timber-framed buildings. The client was the local industrialist Theodore Mander, whose taste for the nostalgic Old English style was typical of his times. Apart from the modern domestic conveniences contained within, Wightwick Manor would have felt reassuringly familiar to a Tudor or Jacobean squire. The house is of interest as an exceptional showcase of Victorian art and design, especially the wealth of original Morris & Co. decorations and furnishings. Among the many splendid Pre-Raphaelite works are two endearing portraits: one of Effie Ruskin by John Everett Millais, who later married the lady after her divorce from the austere John Ruskin, and an idealized, romantic likeness of Jane Morris by her ardent admirer and lover, Dante Gabriel Rossetti.

WOODCHESTER PARK MANSION

William Leigh, builder of this Gothic retreat in the heart of rural Gloucestershire, was a Roman Catholic convert who sought to combine his religious mission with a house for living in. The son of a Liverpool merchant, Leigh acquired the Woodchester estate in 1845 and engaged Augustus Welby Northmore Pugin to design his new home. But even the wealthy William Leigh soon found Pugin too expensive and turned to a local man, Benjamin Bucknall, to realize his dream of a medieval house. Leigh did not want a pastiche, but the real thing. In 1854, Bucknall set about building this 'no-compromise' Gothic abode. Before long, however, economic and practical difficulties became apparent. By 1868 work

ground to a halt and the great project was abandoned. What one sees today is, none the less, still impressive. An imposing range of Gothic buildings with fully functioning gargoyles has weathered more than a century of neglect as a most evocative Victorian ruin. It is an eerie experience to walk into the dining room where never a meal was served, to admire the carved masonry in the vaulted chapel, or to inspect the 'medieval' plumbing of the bathroom. Fascinating, too, is what Woodchester reveals about Victorian building methods. Sections of original scaffolding remain *in situ* or lie scattered about the place, just as they were one day about 130 years ago when the builders downed tools and walked away, sadly never to return.

CARDIFF CASTLE

When the youthful John Patrick Crichton Stuart, 3rd Marquis of Bute, inherited his title and the family fortune, he was able to indulge his insatiable passion for the Middle Ages. In 1865 he teamed up with the architect William Burges, in whom he found a kindred spirit, and set about creating within the ruinous walls of Cardiff Castle a flamboyant piece of medievalist stage scenery. The chivalrous knights and fair ladies portrayed in colourful settings of history and legend are lighter in touch than most Victorian productions of the Gothic Revival. It is perhaps the sheer theatricality that makes the Bute-Burges work at Cardiff Castle so entertaining and overwhelming in its effect.

CASTELL COCH

Even before work at Cardiff Castle was complete, Lord Bute and William Burges set their sights on a fresh medievalist project. For the nearby ruins of Castell Coch ('Red Castle'), a small thirteenth-century fortification, Burges proposed a comprehensive restoration as 'a Country residence for . . . occasional occupation in the Summer'. The result was a bizarre creation, outwardly resembling something from medieval France. The riotous interior, completed after the death of Burges in 1881, is a hybrid affair. Lady Bute's bedroom feels like an oriental seraglio, where French Gothic mingles with Moorish exotica. The drawing room is adorned with a menagerie of beasts, including a monkey with Darwinian beard. In keeping with the best tradition of aristocratic follies, Castell Coch was hardly ever used.

WADDESDON MANOR

A dash of French fantasy erupted in the Buckinghamshire hills in 1874, when Baron Ferdinand de Rothschild commissioned Gabriel-Hippolyte Destailleur to build a Renaissance-style château at Waddesdon. With the interiors, Baron Ferdinand aimed for a pure and thorough re-creation of eighteenth-century French style by using authentic materials to construct the rooms as they would have appeared in their original settings. The grounds also received the full treatment, with a rococo aviary and a genuine Italian baroque fountain featuring Pluto and Proserpina, acquired from the ducal palace at Colorno near Parma. Rothschild clearly considered it pointless to build a second-rate copy

when the real thing could be bought outright. Mindful of its regular hunting and shooting guests, the Bachelors' Wing offered all the creature comforts of a smoking room and billiard room, which are as quintessentially English as any gentleman's club of the period. Sadly, the childless Baron feared that his beautiful creation would fall into decay. In 1897, the year before he died, he wrote: 'May the day yet be distant when weeds will spread over the garden, the terraces crumble into dust, the pictures and cabinets cross the Channel or the Atlantic, and the melancholy cry of the night-jar sound from the deserted towers.' Baron Ferdinand need not have worried about the future of the Manor: Waddesdon is now in the safe hands of the National Trust.

ORIENTAL VISIONS

Victorian nostalgia knew no territorial limits. Although home-grown Gothic was the most popular style, patrons and architects also explored the ancient cultures of the Orient. The Alhambra Court of the Crystal Palace was the most public display of British orientalism, but behind the closed doors of private houses there were many exotic expressions of a lavish kind. After his travels in the East and his acquisition of a considerable collection of Islamic ceramics, Lord Leighton was at a loss to know where to store it. He turned to his friend George Aitchison, who had designed his studio-residence in Kensington, for ideas. Aitchison duly came up with an appropriate design, which used the collection to good effect. Thus

came into being the Arab Hall of Leighton House, completed between 1877 and 1879. This may have influenced the outlandish Arab Hall in Cardiff Castle of 1880 (*right*), the magnificent creation of William Burges for the 3rd Marquis of Bute. Since Burges and Aitchison were friends, the cross-fertilization seems more than likely. It is thought that Burges, whose preferred style was Gothic, derived his ideas from a series of French engravings of seventh-to-eighteenth-century Islamic monuments in Cairo. The Arab Hall was among the last of the interiors in Cardiff Castle on which Burges worked, right up to his death in 1881. Fittingly, Bute had a memorial inscription to his favourite architect carved on the chimneypiece.

URBAN CHALLENGE

In his book *Visits to Remarkable Places* of 1842, the author W Howitt praised Newcastle in glowing terms, writing: 'You walk into what has long been termed the coal hole of the North and find yourself at once in a city of palaces; a fairyland of newness, brightness and modern elegance. And who has wrought this change? It is Mr Grainger.' The classical-style rebirth of Newcastle was indeed the work of the local builder and developer Richard Grainger, who, at the very dawn of the Victorian era, set in train, together with his preferred architect John Dobson, the miracle transformation of his native city on the Tyne. From the foot of Grey's Monument, which surveys the sweeping vista of the noble frontages of Grey Street, one may still admire the fruits of their labours.

Grainger Town, as this central part of Newcastle has come to be generally known, was somewhat ahead of its time in design terms. Most other great industrial towns of the period were still in the early stages of unplanned, anarchic growth, and the urban boom was widely regarded with a hand-wringing mixture of horror and fascination. John Ruskin's much quoted condemnation of London as the 'great foul city' was a typically Victorian view of cities in general: 'rattling, growling, smoking, stinking – a ghastly heap of fermenting brick-work, pouring out poison at every pore'. Overwhelming as London undoubtedly was, students of the Victorian city generally focus their attention further north to come to grips with the urban phenomenon.

One particular northern city, Manchester, came to be regarded as the very symbol of the new age. In 1839 General Napier described it as 'the entrance to hell realized!'; while the future prime minister Benjamin Disraeli, following his visit there in 1843, wrote of 'the most wonderful city of modern times'. However contrasting their views, most commentators tended to agree on one thing – this booming city of manufacture stood in the vanguard of urban progress. Whatever happened here today would repeat itself elsewhere tomorrow. For better or for worse, the future was Manchester.

Manchester's post-industrial decline has long concealed the genuine virtues of the place. But the recent phase of regeneration now allows us to look at the city with new eyes. Nowadays, when a sudden burst of sunshine dispels the grey Mancunian clouds and illuminates the Rochdale Canal against a backdrop of clear blue sky, the formerly neglected façades of the red-brick warehouses are transformed into those exotic Italianate palazzi that inspired their creators; and once again we are able to share the vision of the founding fathers. For a taste of Victorian Manchester, there is a great vista from the mock-Venetian setting of Southmill Street towards the imposing Gothic of Alfred Waterhouse's Manchester Town Hall of 1869, whose tower is poised like a space rocket, primed for take-off.

Just like the Flemish cities of the Middle Ages, Britain's Victorian cities vied with one another to erect the most lavish civic buildings. There are magnificent examples of the genre in Rochdale, Halifax, Middlesbrough, Bradford, Sheffield and Glasgow, as well as those scattered among the boroughs of London. One of the most remarkable is Leeds Town Hall of 1855–59, designed by Cuthbert Brodrick. This vast wedding cake in the classical manner gives an insight into what drove the Victorians to invest so heavily in enormously expensive status symbols. The huge cost was justified in part by the argument that such a noble building would inspire the local population to glimpse a higher realm of art and beauty, one that would lift them out of their humble surroundings.

Victorian civic buildings continue their mission of moral uplift. St George's Hall, Liverpool, by Harvey Lonsdale Elmes, still stands on its commanding plateau, possessing all the self-assurance of a Parthenon on its Acropolis. The *Illustrated London News* hailed its opening in 1854: 'This magnificent edifice will be a perennial monument of the energy and public spirit . . . of the people of Liverpool; a place . . . which, in the quick yet solid growth of its commercial greatness, surpasses even the metropolis itself.' Likewise, the majestic Town Hall and Council House in Birmingham frame one of the most splendid Victorian cityscapes in the country.

The boom cities of the nineteenth century spawned wondrous facilities from grand hotels, railway stations and theatres to covered markets and shopping arcades. Among the very best of their kind are the Leeds City Markets and the nearby County Arcade. Grainger Market in Newcastle was once considered to rank with the best in Europe. Inside, a Marks & Spencer original Penny Bazaar shopfront still survives, with its early gas lamps and gilt red-glass fascia. There was also an outpouring of elegant street furniture, such as the distinctive benches and dolphin lampposts in London along the Embankment.

Manchester Town Hall, a nostalgic Gothic design of 1869 by Alfred Waterhouse for a progressive industrial city, ranks as one of the greatest monuments of the Victorian era. The imposing edifice makes the most of its prominent city-centre location on Albert Square, which displays its own smaller version of an Albert Memorial along with various statues of Victorian worthies. The interior of the building is no less impressive than its grandiose exterior. Solid virtues prevail in the circular staircases of granite and the heavy vaults that support the tremendous weight of the structure.

The magnificent Great Hall is remarkable not only on account of its stately proportions but also for the famous murals, painted by Ford Madox Brown over a period of fifteen years. Originally hailed as one of the wonders of the age and a proud symbol of municipal pride, Manchester Town Hall has had to weather the storms of changing fashion. In the 1950s it was even suggested by some critics that the building should be demolished and replaced with something contemporary. Today, this Victorian Gothic *tour de force* is a proud landmark of modern Manchester.

The rampant growth in industry resulted in the creation of model factory towns, such as Saltaire near Bradford in Yorkshire, Port Sunlight on Merseyside and Bournville in Birmingham. As early as the 1840s, the Great Western Railway commenced building the Swindon Railway Village. Middlesbrough, however, can rightly claim to be the world's first railway town, in the strictest sense of the term, since there was nothing on this greenfield site in 1829, apart from a few farm buildings, when the owners of the Stockton & Darlington extended the line to this more convenient point for shipping coal down the Tees.

Middlesbrough also provides us with an object lesson in the ruthless dynamics of Victorian urbanism. Gladstone declared on his visit there in 1862: 'This remarkable place, the youngest child of England's enterprise . . . is an infant, gentlemen, but it is an infant Hercules.' The original town hall in which he made his speech is now abandoned, marooned in a semi-derelict landscape some distance from the modern town centre. The reason for this occurrence was the opening of a second railway station, which left the original settlement on the wrong side of the tracks. Attempting to seek out the earliest relics of Middlesbrough's unique Victorian heritage is, thus, something of a journey of discovery to challenge the enthusiast.

But whatever attractions Victorian cities offered, the well-to-do always preferred leafy suburbia. Leeds had its Headingley, Newcastle its Jesmond and Birmingham its Edgbaston, all within easy reach of the bright lights but well away from the noise and the filth that blighted the lives of millions of urbanites. London had not only its Holland Park and Bedford Park but plenty of other salubrious areas as well. In this respect, as in others, the metropolis stands apart from the rest.

However, it is the boom Victorian cities, such as Glasgow, Manchester, Birmingham, Leeds and Liverpool, that offer the most authentic, undiluted urban experience of the nineteenth century. But for all their undoubted achievements in building and improving cities, the Victorians seemed to take up the urban challenge with a sense of duty rather than any real enthusiasm. Their hearts were in the fast-vanishing countryside.

Dolphin lampposts adorn the Embankment built between 1868 and 1874 by Sir Joseph Bazalgette over London's new main drainage system.

Broad Street, Birmingham – a Victorian streetscape that offers a vision of Venice built in Midlands redbrick.

39 HARRINGTON GARDENS, LONDON

This flamboyant creation by Ernest George was built between 1882 and 1883 as the centrepiece of a row of speculative houses in Kensington that were clearly intended for people who wanted to stand out in a crowd. In this spectacular development, the architect carried out a wholesale transfer of decorative features copied from the rich burghers' houses he had sketched in Bruges, Amsterdam and Ghent, in order to enliven the customary uniformity of the London streetscape. Appropriately, the first occupant of 39 Harrington Gardens turned out to be W S Gilbert, the librettist of the Gilbert and Sullivan comic operas, who was perhaps attracted by the powerful theatrical appearance of the place. He lived here from 1883 until 1890.

HOLLAND PARK, LONDON

This street displays the 'Kensington Italianate' grand manner, which was the preferred style for the upper classes in Victorian London. Although the general trend was overwhelmingly for Gothic with regard to public buildings, the palazzo model continued to exert a powerful appeal for domestic architecture. The noble frontages, stately avenues and leafy squares of districts such as Holland Park and Notting Hill, developed from the 1860s onwards, represent some of the most impressive examples of Victorian urban elegance. Originally designed as individual houses, such dwellings were veritable bastions for the very rich. Nowadays, there might be up to sixteen different doorbells for all the flats and studios contained in such grand establishments, where previously just one family would have resided.

HOLBORN VIADUCT, LONDON

A fine example of Victorian urban improvement, Holborn Viaduct was designed by City Surveyor William Heywood and completed in 1869. This quarter-of-a-mile-long roadbridge spared the horses the strenuous descent and ascent of the Fleet valley. The utilitarian structure is adorned with allegorical figures representing Commerce, Agriculture, Science and Fine Art. The approaches were originally flanked by four distinctive buildings. Two of these survive, still with their statues of City worthies in elegant niches. Work on the Holborn Viaduct lasted for six years and cost the phenomenal sum for those days of £2.5 million. As was usual with such major schemes, thousands of people were made homeless in the process.

PEABODY BUILDINGS, LONDON

One of the great heroes of ordinary Victorian Londoners was the American philanthropist George Peabody, who endowed a fund with £500,000 of his personal fortune 'to ameliorate the condition of the poor and needy of this great metropolis and to promote their comfort and happiness'. Replacing slums with 'cheap, cleanly, well-drained and healthful dwellings for the poor' became the main objective of the Peabody Donation Fund. The first Peabody Building went up in Commercial Street, Spitalfields, between 1862 and 1864. The austere, prison-like design by H A Darbishire was the model for many other blocks all over London. By 1890, more than 5,000 separate living units had been created. This example in Bloomsbury is typical of the Peabody Buildings, clearly intended to offer a haven of respectability in the sea of urban deprivation still lapping at the doorstep.

ROYAL ARCADE, LONDON

The use of glass in construction, which was spectacularly pioneered in the Crystal Palace at the Great Exhibition and many railway stations, also found an ideal application in the bright, new shopping arcades that were springing up in towns and cities all over the country. One such is the Royal Arcade of 1879, which runs between Albemarle Street and Old Bond Street in London. Perhaps on account of its proximity to Buckingham Palace, Queen Victoria used to shop in the Royal Arcade, buying her handkerchiefs, riding shirts, vests and knitting wool from a shop formerly at number 12. The two entrance façades of the Royal Arcade are brash and fanciful in a typically Victorian way, which has not always found favour with the architectural purists.

LEADENHALL MARKET, LONDON

This unassuming structure in the heart of the City of London is a very pleasing Victorian creation, in which architecture and engineering come together in perfect harmony. Designed in 1881 by Horace Jones, the official architect of the City, the buildings occupy the site of a market for poultry and dairy products that took its name from the fourteenth-century mansion with a lead roof belonging to the Neville family. The Leadenhall Market is still in business, a rare reminder of the everyday needs of the many Londoners once living in the Square Mile – an area now given over almost entirely to finance and commerce. Note the coat of arms of the City of London on the plinth of the column.

CITY CHAMBERS, GLASGOW

This grand building, designed by William Young, represents the very summit of municipal architecture in Scotland. The exterior, dominated by a mighty Renaissance-style tower, is a riot of French, Flemish and Venetian motifs. The interior is even more lavish. The loggia, grand staircase and reception rooms are a powerful expression of Victorian opulence. Italian marble, Spanish mahogany, stained glass, ceramic tiles, mural paintings and alabaster friezes combine to dazzle the eye. First conceived soon after Glasgow's major financial crisis of 1878, the City Chambers were partly intended as a means of boosting commercial morale. Some critics carped that the opulence of the building went too far. As such, however, it is a perfect reflection of Victorian Glasgow, and Queen Victoria inaugurated this majestic status symbol of the 'Second City of Empire' in 1888.

TOWN HALL, BIRMINGHAM

This amazing structure, designed by Joseph Aloysius Hansom, the inventor of the famous cab that bears his name, was opened in 1834 and extended in 1837. Its resoundingly neo-classical style clearly marks it out as a product from the very beginning of the Victorian era, before the Gothic revival had swept aside all competing styles. Modelled on the Temple of Castor and Pollux in Rome, Birmingham Town Hall is surrounded by some forty massive Corinthian columns. In spite of its name, this grand civic building was not intended for municipal administration but as a multi-purpose venue for meetings, functions and concerts.

SWINDON RAILWAY VILLAGE

When the Great Western Railway decided to locate its headquarters in Swindon, it sparked off an urban explosion in the small Wiltshire town. The pre-railway population of little more than 1,000 in 1840 jumped to 7,000 by 1861 and then doubled again in the course of the next decade. In order to accommodate the massive influx of workers, the GWR built a model village laid out on a gridiron pattern of eight streets, which took their names from stations served by the company, such as Bath, Bristol, Exeter and Taunton. In all, some 300 railway cottages were built, offering considerable comfort by the standards of the time. These are still occupied, although the one at 34 Farringdon Road has been restored to how things looked at the turn of the century.

PORT SUNLIGHT

William Hesketh Lever was a self-made man who expanded his family grocery business into a hugely successful concern by turning Sunlight Soap into a best-selling brand. A man of firm Nonconformist principles, Lever had a vision of creating an ideal community for his workforce. When he relocated to a new factory on Merseyside, Lever seized the opportunity to realize his dream. The result was Port Sunlight, founded in 1888, a place where Lever hoped his workers would experience a more enriching existence than that offered by the usual humdrum routine of daily drudgery. The brave social experiment that was Port Sunlight still looks attractive enough with its green spaces and neat houses full of vernacular features. The social vision of the founding father lingers on.

HARD GRAFT

A row of cottages from Merthyr Tydfil in Wales, re-erected at the Museum of Welsh Life St Fagan's, documents the domestic lifestyle of ironworkers in the nineteenth century.

Perhaps the favourite motto of the Victorian era was *Labor Omnia Vincit*. In Leeds Town Hall, the city fathers thoughtfully added an English translation: Industry Overcomes All Things. This simple idea was a fixed tenet of Victorian faith. Work was the answer to everything. Palmerston, in a famous speech in1865, encouraged his south London audience with a stirring promise: 'Wealth is . . . within the reach of all . . . you will by systematic industry, raise yourselves in the social system . . . acquire honour and respect . . .' Even Thomas Carlyle, the leading social philosopher of the age, who blamed the nation's spiritual decline on 'the cash nexus of man with man', saw salvation to lie in the general acceptance of a severe work ethic. So whichever way one chooses to look at it, whether for material progress or for moral redemption, this was an age that elevated hard graft to a quasi-religious principle.

From our modern perspective, the factories of the textile industry, with their floor upon floor of water- and steam-powered looms clattering at a near-deafening pitch, most clearly evoke the working life of the times. However, the textile industry was not a Victorian invention. Establishments such as Quarry Bank Mill, near Manchester, were founded in the Georgian period, but typically it was the introduction here of steam in 1836, coupled with a mechanization of production, that literally gave power to the industrial revolution. The great steam engines of the Victorian era, with their massive wheels and pistons in motion, still present an awesome sight. They performed a variety of essential tasks: whether driving looms in Bradford, hoisting coal and miners in Wales, or delivering drinking water from pumping stations in London.

The mills and factories best express the super-human ambitions and presumptions of the Victorian age. Disraeli described the sort of things to be seen around Cottonopolis, as Manchester was then known: '. . . illumined factories with more windows than Italian palaces and smoking chimneys taller than Italian obelisks.' Among the many exotic creations of this genre are the stunningly authentic Egyptian-style Temple Mill in Leeds and the palatial Bliss Mill at Chipping Norton, Oxfordshire.

What possessed the cost-conscious Victorian industrialists to spend so copiously on these extravagant monuments? On one level, they can be construed as flashy status symbols of competing capitalists boasting of their success and proclaiming one-upmanship. But they also celebrate the general triumph of the new order, in which the promise of social advancement through industry was gloriously fulfilled. However, while admiring the architectural glories of Victorian industry, it is as well not to forget the plight of the working population, the masses that supplied the sweated labour.

Manchester was but one of many cities that provided those scenes of urban squalor, scenes that gave Friedrich Engels so much material for his book *Condition of the Working Class in England*. Countless thousands of young lives were wrecked by shocking maltreatment in the workplace, as movingly described by Frances Trollope, mother of the novelist Anthony Trollope, in *The Life and Adventures of Michael Armstrong, the Factory Boy*: 'Even at dead of night the machinery was never stopped and when one set of fainting children were dragged from the mules another set were dragged from the reeking beds they were about to occupy in order to take their places.'

Not all employers were the same, however – there were some with a social conscience. The moral lessons of Robert Owen in New Lanark were taken up by succeeding generations of philanthropically minded entrepreneurs, who established model working communities. These included: Sir Titus Salt in Saltaire, George Cadbury at Bournville and William Hesketh Lever at Port Sunlight. And nor were all manufacturing endeavours on the massive scale associated with those dark, satanic mills of legendary repute. Stott Park Bobbin Mill in Cumbria, for example, which supplied the textile industry throughout the Victorian era and beyond, looks like a pleasant enough place to work, set within the rugged splendour of the Lake District. But conditions here were tough and dangerous in their own way, and this was not all that far from Brantwood, where John Ruskin had sought refuge from the evils of the industrial age.

Mining was also of paramount importance during this era. The Black Country Museum at Dudley tells the story of the highly prized seam of Staffordshire Thick Coal that provided a livelihood for many thousands of workers in the Midlands. The abandoned engine houses dotting Cornwall's landscape are evocative relics of the tin mines that made the county a

Temple Mill in Leeds, built between 1838 and 1843, was designed by Joseph Bonomi as a faithful copy of a genuine Egyptian temple at Edfu.

Order and discipline are the obvious hallmarks of Saltaire, the model industrial community built by Bradford mill owner Sir Titus Salt between 1851 and 1871. In stark contrast to the insalubrious and overcrowded slums where most ordinary folk were condemned to live, Salt's workers could enjoy the essential benefits of open-ended streets and well ventilated houses. But the price they paid for these amenities of contemporary civilization was in leading lives regimented at the discretion of their philanthropic master. While the debate continues as to the web of obligations involved in this relationship of dependency, the genuine urban values of such model settlements as Saltaire are now generally acknowledged as being ahead of their time.

buzzing hive of industry in the last century. However, there is virtually no sign remaining today of the 'mine of mines' exploited by the Devon Great Consols, which supplied a bonanza of top-grade copper lode between 1844 and 1903. The volume of the enterprise may be judged from the extensive remains of Morwellham Quay on the River Tamar, from where the valuable cargo was shipped.

Some of the most evocative Victorian industrial sites are those in remote places that, having had their moment of glory, have sunk back into graceful oblivion. One such is the flooded slate quarries of Easdale Island off the coast of Argyllshire. Here, on a strip of land

Easdale Island, off the west coast of Scotland, is one of the most fascinating sites of industrial archaeology. In its Victorian heyday this remote spot was a slate production centre of worldwide renown. When the inland quarries were exhausted, attention turned to those running into the sea. Deep channels were cut and each sealed with a lock gate. The flooded slate quarries, dating from the nineteenth century, now present an eerie spectacle. The abandoned workings bear witness to the hard toil of several generations. Easdale slate was once a valuable export that found its way to all corners of the globe, from Canada and Jamaica to America and Australia. Among notable Scottish buildings roofed with Easdale slate figure Iona Abbey and Stalker Castle.

This well-preserved group of kilns, which once produced industrial lime for cement, can be seen at the Black Country Museum, Dudley.

only 650 yards long by 500 yards wide, a population of 450 people lived and worked in 1839. The community prospered until 1881, when a violent storm filled the slate workings with seawater. The place never recovered and the quarries of Easdale Island finally ceased production altogether in 1911. Many of the former china clay pits of Cornwall have also been flooded – the only reminder of these former industrial sites being the lurid waters of surreal green and blue that remain to enliven the landscape.

Office work also abounded for the armies of clerks who were needed to administer the industries, railways, banks, insurance houses and a host of other companies that were springing up all over the country. Commerce demanded palatial buildings. The merchants' premises in Bradford's Little Germany are styled like Roman palazzi. Alfred Waterhouse's Prudential Assurance in High Holborn, London, built in 1899 resembles a Gothic castle worthy of Ludwig II of Bavaria. The same architect's design of 1890 for the Refuge Assurance Company in Manchester was an even more extravagant concoction, finding space within its structure for a magnificent ballroom. This building has recently found a new lease of life, aptly renamed as the Palace Hotel.

White-collar workers were subject to the same strict work ethic as their manual colleagues. A 'Notice to Employees' dated 1852 and addressed to the clerical staff of a Burnley cotton mill conceded that henceforth the working day would be only from 7am to 6pm, with the partaking of lunch permitted between 11.30am and noon – this concession of lunch was conditional that work did not on any account cease. The notice ended with a telling remark: 'The owners recognize the generosity of the new Labour Laws, but will expect a great rise in the output of work to compensate for these near utopian conditions.' Hard graft was indeed the undisputed order of the day.

CORNISH TIN

Although the extraction of tin goes back to pre-Roman times, it was during the nineteenth century, with the deployment of the Cornish beam engine, that the industry really took off. At the peak of activity in the 1850s, some 650 beam engines were working in Cornwall alone. But the industry was subject to massive swings of fortune. This, coupled with starvation wages and appalling working conditions, prompted countless Cornish miners to try their luck all over the world, from Australia and California to South America. After the 1870s, the general trend was one of steady decline. Today, the map of Cornwall is littered with the 'knacked bals', or disused mines, bearing resonant names such as Ding Dong, Levant

and Wheal Prosper. Perched on the rugged cliffs of the Cornish coast the ruinous engine houses at Towanroath and Botallack are no more than empty shells, and the unnatural silence is broken only by the wind whistling in their tall, round chimneys. But Cornwall's real tin-mining heritage lies hidden underground in hundreds of miles of shafts and tunnels painfully excavated by hand. Many workings extend far out beneath the sea. In these, the miners heard the ceaseless pounding of the mighty Atlantic grinding away the ocean floor above their heads. The National Trust has a number of engine houses in its care, and two fine specimens, complete with their formidable Victorian engines dating from 1887 and 1891, are on show at East Pool near Redruth.

WHEAL MARTYN

Steam power gave a vital boost to the china-clay industry, enabling producers to meet the ever-growing demands of pottery and paper manufacture. In the 1880s, Elias Martyn modernized the existing works at Wheal Martyn, near St Austell, creating the basic layout that can still be seen today. A visitor trail at the Wheal Martyn Museum makes clear the entire production process, as it was in operation more than a century ago, from extraction of the china clay by water pressure, then through the various stages of purification, and finally to the settling pits where the precious raw material was removed as a thick sludge at the bottom of the tanks. After that, the china clay was dried in pan-kilns and either cut into blocks or packed into casks ready for shipment.

MORWELLHAM QUAY

There can be fewer more unlikely industrial sites than the sleepy lower reaches of the River Tamar. It was from Morwellham Quay that the Devon Great Consols exported its copper ore to customers all over the world. At its peak between 1848 and 1858, the Tamar Valley was Europe's main source of copper. The 1850s were Morwellham's boom years, when as much as 4,000 tons of copper ore would be awaiting shipment on the quayside. Model cottages, a school, two chapels and an inn once served this village of 200 people. The decline began soon after 1859, when the Great Western Railway opened a branch line to Tavistock. The final demise gradually set in as the copper deposits were exhausted. By 1901 Morwellham Quay was virtually a ghost town. It has now found a new lease of life as a heritage site.

WELSH BACK GRANARY, BRISTOL

This eye-catching warehouse built in 1869 flaunts an eclectic style that has been aptly described as 'Bristol Byzantine'. The original design was the work of two local architects, Archibald Ponton and W V Gough. The flamboyant exterior displays the polychromatic brickwork that became a distinctive feature of Victorian architecture. Bold structural elements, such as columns and arches, add great power to the surface decoration. The Guelfic battlements, strongly reminiscent of an Italian palazzo in Venice or Florence, add a truly exotic flourish to what was essentially a workaday building.

ABBEY MILL, BRADFORD-ON-AVON

Textile manufacture in the West Country was a traditional industry stretching back to the Middle Ages. However, by the beginning of the nineteenth century, the region had long been overtaken and eclipsed by the great mills of Yorkshire and Lancashire. Abbey Mill, built in 1875, represented a spirited attempt to stage a comeback, although by then the competitive advantages of the North were too great. Local cloth production received a welcome stimulus in the short term, but the mill was never really a viable enterprise. Abbey Mill was converted into offices and a restaurant between 1968 and 1972. The classical façades and elegant fenestration still make a fine display on the banks of the Avon.

MANNINGHAM MILLS, BRADFORD

One of the most imposing industrial buildings ever conceived, the complex of mills constructed by Samuel C Lister in Bradford dates from 1873. Lister was a prolific inventor of new processes in textile manufacture, taking out 150 patents in the course of a busy career. Manningham Mills made use of Lister's revolutionary technique using an improved Spanish loom for turning waste silk into profitable products such as velvet and plush. A lofty chimney above the boiler house, disguised as an Italian campanile, crowns the ensemble. The looming presence of such a monumental building dominated not only the skyline but also the mental horizons of the workforce living in much humbler style within walking distance of the factory gates.

TEMPLETON'S CARPET FACTORY, GLASGOW

This outlandish building in Glasgow is arguably the most exotic of industrial edifices. Its heady mix of Venetian Gothic, Romanesque, multi-coloured mosaics and polychrome brickwork conspires to dazzle the eye. The general effect, reminiscent of a Turkish textile design, once served to advertise the wares of Templeton's Carpet Factory, as this stunning creation was formerly known. William Leiper designed it in 1889 for an enterprise that declared its intent 'as patrons of the arts, resolved not alone in the interests of the workers, but also of the citizens, to erect instead of the ordinary and common factory something of permanent architectural interest and beauty'. The general effect was praised in no uncertain terms: '. . . nothing finer is to be found outside of Italy.' This claim would be churlish to dispute for an astounding industrial version of a Doge's Palace.

31 TOAD LANE, ROCHDALE

Individual acts of philanthropy notwithstanding, most Victorian industrialists were inclined to exploit their workforce however they could. In response, the co-operative idea promoted an alternative way forward with a collective system of self-help in order to achieve a fairer distribution of the spoils of labour. As a practical force, the Co-operative Movement dates from the foundation, in 1844, of the Rochdale Equitable Pioneers' Society. Its twenty-eight original members have been immortalized as the Rochdale Pioneers, since they were the first to bring such an operation to a successful outcome. Their original headquarters, a modest warehouse at 31 Toad Lane, is now a fascinating museum, which shows how the strength of a simple idea launched the world-wide Co-operative Movement.

TRENCHERFIELD MILL, WIGAN PIER

Harnessing the power of steam was the key to the industrial miracle of the nineteenth century. The great engines, which kept the factory machines turning, were not only triumphant symbols of the new technology, but also objects of awesome beauty. In common with the practice of naming ships, christening ceremonies were regularly conducted to inaugurate engines, both large and small. One of the most famous manufacturers of the era was John & Edward Wood of Bolton. The firm was also responsible for the magnificent engine at Trencherfield Mill, Wigan Pier, of 1906. At the time, this was the largest engine ever made by the company, so large in fact that the two sides were given separate names: Helen and Rina.

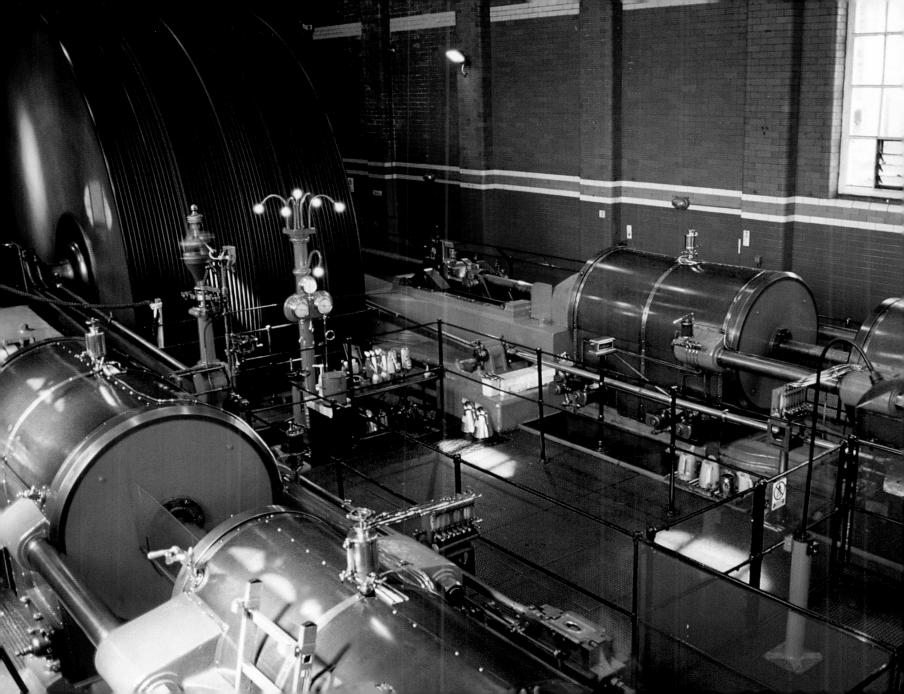

PAPER MILL, WOOKEY HOLE

Papermaking using rags and remnants from textile manufacture provides an early example of industrial recycling. At Wookey Hole in Somerset there is the rare sight of vintage Victorian papermaking equipment still in operation, and working according to the original manufacturing processes. On reaching the mill, the cotton rags were first cut by hand into small segments and then boiled under pressure (to increase the temperature) in a huge cast-iron sphere using caustic soda and lime to soften them and

remove any grease they contained. The resulting 'porridge' was then mashed and beaten before being laid out in wooden frames and dried to create the finished product. With industrial production methods rapidly changing according to the relentless forces of technological progress and modernization in the nineteenth century, the survival of the paper mill at Wookey Hole is particularly remarkable. This working example of Victorian manufacturing, albeit on a modest scale, is a valuable time capsule, one that opens a small window on the past.

ON THE MOVE

The Forth Railway Bridge, opened in 1890, was hailed by *The Times* as the 'greatest feat of engineering that the world has ever seen'.

The railway age received a huge boost on 13 June 1842 when Queen Victoria became the first reigning British monarch ever to travel by train. Her journey took her from Slough to Paddington, and she declared herself to be 'quite charmed' by the experience. Over the next six decades, Victoria was a constant patron of the rampant rail network. A number of luxurious royal trains were built for her personal use. Her favourite carriage, dating from 1895 when two separate ones of 1869 vintage were joined together, has found a permanent siding at the National Railway Museum in York. The Queen's Suite in this veritable palace on wheels boasts a plush interior lined with red and white silk and gilded fittings worthy of the Empress of India.

The Stockton & Darlington had led the way in 1825, but fully fledged passenger railways really date from 1830 with the Liverpool & Manchester. The effect on the general public was nothing less than phenomenal. Actress Fanny Kemble hailed the train as 'a magical machine, with its flying white breath and rhythmical, unvarying pace'. With her eyes closed, she felt as if she were actually flying. Lord Tennyson was so moved by his trip on the railway that he composed his famous line: 'Let the great world spin for ever down the ringing grooves of change.' The poet, who had been travelling by night, could not see that the train wheels actually ran on rails.

Passenger comfort in the early years of the system was at a premium. First class enjoyed upholstered seats but no heating, while second class had to endure bare wooden benches, and third class had not even a roof. Furthermore, the builders of the world's first passenger railway had absolutely no idea of what a station should look like. For example, Manchester's Liverpool Road Station of 1830, now part of the Museum of Science & Industry, resembled a normal late-Georgian streetscape. But as the many-tentacled octopus spread its iron rails to all corners of the land – 6,000 miles of track being laid between 1825 and 1850 – the railway station evolved into the great symbolic monument of the age.

In architectural terms alone, the Victorian station was truly impressive. The refurbished Gothic fantasia of St Pancras of 1868–74 or the former glory of the Greek Revival doric arch at Euston of 1838, contrasting as they were, both expressed the huge excitement of the railway age. But the real miracle lay behind the magnificent façades, in the revolutionary engineering of the train sheds, which were at the cutting edge of contemporary design technology. The great curved structures of iron and glass at York or Newcastle were the true cathedrals of the age. They still have a powerful effect well over a century later.

As the railways extended their networks, vested interests put up stiff opposition. Aristocratic apprehensions were voiced by the Duke of Wellington, alarmed that the lower classes would be encouraged 'to move about'. Oxford University feared that the railway would endanger the morals of the students. The landed gentry looked on with horror as their country estates were violated by gangs of common labourers laying tracks, although the pain was often assuaged by financial compensation. The threat of a nasty future, with locomotives steaming through England's green and pleasant land, rumbles on in the novels of Thomas Hardy and George Eliot. Thomas Carlyle warned in customary apocalyptic terms of small towns 'confusedly waltzing, in a state of progressive dissolution, towards the four winds; and know not where the end of the death-dance will be for them'. Morris dismissed the Forth Railway Bridge as 'the supremest specimen of ugliness'.

Such fears are among the reasons why railway stations were often confined to the edges of towns. Prohibitive costs were another. London did not acquire a single central station, but a number of peripheral ones perched on the fringes. Marylebone was the fifteenth of these termini when it opened in 1899. Transferring between stations caused chronic traffic congestion, and this was why the Metropolitan Railway was built in 1863 from Paddington to Farringdon. The original brick vaults of what later became the Circle Line can still be seen at stations such as Baker Street and Great Portland Street.

For most Victorians, however, it was railway euphoria. The mood was epitomized by Brunel's Great Western Railway, the *crème de la crème* of the private companies. The GWR, or 'God's Wonderful Railway', saw itself as being a cut above the others. Its adherence to the 7ft Broad Gauge, when the rest of the country had the 4ft 8½in Standard Gauge, meant that the GWR had to seek gentler gradients for its routes. This brought it the nickname of the 'Great Way Round'. But even the GWR had to bow to the inevitable when, in 1892, it finally scrapped the Broad Gauge. Sections of the sacred track are preserved at the Didcot Railway Centre,

An authentic Victorian railway station has been faithfully rebuilt at the North of England Open Air Museum, Beamish.

where a working replica of the Firefly class of Broad Gauge locomotive has been constructed. This design of 1839 by Daniel Gooch held the world speed record in the 1860s. It was behind such a locomotive that Victoria took her first ride in a train.

This impressive replica of a train of the Liverpool & Manchester Railway is on show at the National Railway Museum in York.

The railway system eventually took away most of the commercial traffic for which the extensive canal network had been built from the last quarter of the eighteenth century. But the canal age had one glorious late flourish in the Manchester Ship Canal of 1894, with which Mancunian businessmen sought to circumvent the high harbour dues charged by Liverpool. As for travel on the high seas, the *Cutty Sark*, the world's last surviving clipper ship, was already one of an endangered species when she entered service in 1869. Steam and iron were fast replacing sail and wood. But the definitive technological breakthrough occurred in 1894, when *Turbinia*, barely 104 feet long, built by Charles Parsons on Tyneside, demonstrated the awesome power of the steam-turbine. The experiment was a huge success. In 1901, a Clyde passenger vessel was fitted with steam-turbines. Before very long, transatlantic liners such as *Mauretania* and *Lusitania* had followed suit. The original *Turbinia* is on display in Newcastle's Discovery Museum.

In 1860 Europe's first horse-drawn tramway opened in Birkenhead. In 1901 electric trams, such as this example of a double-decker, were introduced.

The Victorian transport revolution was a broad-based one, encompassing everything from electric trams to the first aviation experiments, conducted in the 1890s. At the same time, the postal service and telephone and wireless transmissions created a new type of mobility, which allowed people to send ideas and information ever faster and further. The motor car, too, made its debut right at the end of the century. Victoria was not at all impressed, stating that: 'They smell exceedingly nasty, and are very shaky and disagreeable conveyances altogether.' However, the Victorian era is remembered above all as the Railway Age. Fittingly, the Queen's last journey was by train, when the Great Western Railway brought her body from Paddington to Windsor for burial on 2 February 1901. The wreath of white flowers and the black ribbon that adorned the Royal Sovereign locomotive on that occasion remains a treasured possession of the Swindon Railway Heritage Centre.

STOCKTON & DARLINGTON RAILWAY

The railway age was launched on 27 September 1825 when an enthusiastic crowd clambered into open coal wagons to celebrate the inaugural trip on the Stockton & Darlington. The line, built to transport coal from the Whitton Colliery via Darlington to Stockton for shipment down the Tees, was later extended to Middlesbrough. Stephenson's *Locomotion*, which hauled the first train, is now on display in the Darlington Railway Centre and Museum, located in the renovated North Road passenger station of 1842. This vintage machine made history by being the first steam locomotive to transport passengers on a public railway. In the early days, passengers provided their own conveyances, which were

pulled either by horse or behind locomotives supplied by the railway company. *Locomotion*, which looks rather like a naked boiler on wheels, offered its driver a precarious perch on a narrow running board that was totally exposed to the weather. Also on show are some examples of original rolling stock dating from 1846. Each railway carriage, consisting of three compartments, clearly resembles three individual stagecoaches joined together. The luggage was carried on the roof, and the stark contrast between First Class and Second Class corresponded to the old inside and outside comfort difference of the stagecoach. Even the livery was reminiscent of the old days of the fast-vanishing era of horse-drawn travel.

BUILT in 1846
by
Messrs HORNER and WILKINSON
COMMERCIAL STREET DARLINGTON
for
THE STOCKTON and DARLINGTON RLY COY.

FIRST CLASS

ISLE OF WIGHT
STEAM RAILWAY

The steam locomotive *Freshwater*, which was originally built for the London, Brighton & South Coast Railway in 1876, first came to the Isle of Wight in 1913. This was just one of many antiquated engines and carriages that were brought to the island over the years after having served out their normal working lives on various mainland railways. The Isle of Wight Steam Railway has managed to preserve several of these. Among the impressive collection of ancient rolling stock figure three fully working steam locomotives and four rebuilt carriages of genuine Victorian vintage. These still operate on a scenic five-mile stretch of the former Ryde to Cowes line, which connects with the present-day rail network at Smallbrook Junction.

TORRE STATION, TORQUAY

The Great Western Railway opened up the relatively isolated counties of the West Country. The line reached Exeter in 1844 and then pushed further into Devon and Cornwall, with branch lines down to the coast, putting such seaside towns as Teignmouth on the traveller's map. Much survives of Brunel's Temple Meads Station in Bristol, site of the company's original headquarters, which displays a curious version of the Tudor Revival style. Elsewhere, the GWR built less pretentiously and less nostalgically, but always with a certain distinction. The pleasing blend of iron and wood at Torre Station in Torquay is characteristic of the pioneering days of the Great Western Railway.

St Pancras Station, London

With railway companies vying for supremacy, especially in the 'Race to the North', the style of the London terminii became a serious matter of high-profile publicity. Euston having opted for Greek Doric and Kings Cross for functional Italianate, the Midland Railway allowed George Gilbert Scott to indulge his Gothic fantasies to the full. St Pancras Station of 1868–74, fronted by the Midland Grand Hotel, was the triumphant result. Scott wrote of it ambivalently: 'It is often spoken of to me as the finest building in London, my own belief is that it is possibly too good for its purpose.' Some critics thought Scott had debased noble Gothic for a common, commercial purpose. As with most Victorian stations, the historical façade gives no clue as to the engineering marvel of the great train shed concealed behind.

Liverpool Street Station, London

The western train shed of Liverpool Street Station, built in 1875, displays a perfect fusion of engineering and design. At the time of its opening, it was acclaimed as 'decidedly the most successful attempt to combine iron and brick construction to be seen in London'. It prompted *Building News* to examine the basic Victorian reluctance to consider engineering and architecture as equal partners: 'Our metropolitan terminii have been the leaders of the art-spirit of our times, however loath we may be to admit it, and despite our declaring them to be the work of engineers without artistic merit except of the lowest order.' The issue has since been settled. A Greater London Council report of 1976 referred to the undeniable cathedral-like qualities of Liverpool Street Station.

INLAND WATERWAYS

The canal network, which was largely completed during the Georgian period, continued to function throughout the Victorian era. Ironically, the canals received a timely boost by transporting heavy materials for building the very railways that eventually rendered them obsolete. The distinctive 'Roses and Castles' decoration of the narrow boats, which first evolved during the 1840s and 1850s, was thus very much a Victorian invention. This rich and colourful folk art is still practised today. A fine example is the *Northwich*, built at Saltley, Birmingham, in 1898 as a horse-drawn narrow boat, now permanently moored in Gloucester Docks at the National Waterways

Museum. Other narrow boats displaying traditional decoration are on show at the Canal Museum at Stoke Bruerne, Northamptonshire. Although the leisurely pace and open-air lifestyle of the canals would appear to offer a pleasant alternative to the grim regime of the industrial towns, conditions on the narrow boats were not exactly idyllic. W H King, a canal stalwart all his life, told the story of how his father was stolen as an eight-year-old boy from the family boat and forced to work for three hard years, virtually as a child slave. Although generally locked in a cabin and with no trousers to wear, he eventually managed to escape and went on to set himself up in business as an operator of canal boats.

SADDLEWORTH VIADUCT

The railway age met up with the canal age in the 1840s, when the Saddleworth Viaduct was built to carry the Huddersfield to Manchester line over the Huddersfield Narrow Canal. The dramatic sweep of the mighty structure across the Tame Valley was achieved by skewing the arches so that they appear to twist across the span. This great work, requiring considerable skill from both the engineers and stone masons, is still in service – an enduring Victorian feature that dominates the landscape for miles around in this rugged moorland setting.

Barton Aqueduct

When the Manchester Ship Canal was built in the 1890s, the crossing with the existing Bridgewater Canal posed a technical problem that was solved in a novel manner. Sir Leader Williams designed an ingenious aqueduct to carry the old canal over the new that could be swung on a central pier through a 90-degree angle, thus enabling large ships to pass by without obstruction. The movable element consists of a steel tank 235 feet long, eighteen feet wide and six feet deep. This sizeable section of the Bridgewater Canal, weighing a massive 1,450 tons, including 800 tons of water, is still in good working order and is rotated every day. The Barton Aqueduct, inaugurated in 1893, remains a fine example of Victorian engineering at its most inventive and resourceful.

ALBERT BRIDGE, LONDON

This three-span structure linking Chelsea and Battersea was originally built to a cantilevered design by Roland Mason Ordish between 1871 and 1873. It was subsequently modified by Joseph Bazalgette in 1884 with the addition of the suspension members. Its highly ornamental style makes something apparently light and graceful out of such heavy materials as wrought and cast iron. Although the roadway had to be strengthened in the 1970s to bear the increasing traffic load, the Albert Bridge continues to cut a decidedly elegant dash across the Thames. The Victorian toll booths remain at either end of the Albert Bridge, which presents a magnificent sight when illuminated at night.

CLIFTON SUSPENSION BRIDGE, BRISTOL

First designed by Isambard Kingdom Brunel, the most famous of the Victorian engineers, in the 1820s, but work on a modified design did not commence until 1831. Then, in 1840, with only the piers *in situ*, money ran out and nothing more was done for twenty years. In the meantime, the chains were sold for Brunel's Royal Albert Bridge over the Tamar at Saltash. Only after the death of Brunel in 1859 were the finances in place for work to continue. Chains were then obtained from the demolished Hungerford Bridge in London. The Clifton Suspension Bridge finally opened in 1864. The monumental brick piers reflect the Egyptian style that was much to Brunel's liking.

SS *GREAT BRITAIN*, BRISTOL

The first plates of the iron keel of a bold new vessel were laid in Bristol as early as 1839. Launched in 1843, Isambard Kingdom Brunel's SS *Great Britain* was the first screw-driven iron ship to cross the Atlantic. The revolutionary design, commissioned by the Great Western Steamship Company, was the largest vessel afloat at the time. The aim of the venture was to wrest back the initiative from the American vessels, which had totally dominated the transatlantic trade for the preceding three decades. After a chequered career, which ended on an ignominious note with her being beached in the Falklands, the SS *Great Britain* was salvaged in 1970 and brought back to the very same Great Western Dry Dock in Bristol where she had been built.

S.S. GREAT BRITAIN

HMS *WARRIOR*, PORTSMOUTH

The world's first iron-hulled battleship, ranking in her day as the largest, fastest and most powerful naval vessel, was built in 1860 as Britain's response to the French iron-clad *La Gloire*. Charles Dickens, a native of Portsmouth where HMS *Warrior* has now found her final berth as a floating museum, described her terrifying effect: 'A black vicious ugly customer as ever I saw, whale-like in size, and with as terrible a row of incisor teeth as ever closed on a French frigate.' One of the last ships to carry a figurehead, a suitably martial portrayal of a mythical warrior with drawn sword and thunderbolts on his shield, HMS *Warrior* proved to be the ultimate deterrent since she never fired a shot in anger. Going down below decks gives visitors a fascinating insight into Victorian naval life, while the combined use of sail and power still offers lessons for shipbuilders today.

ALBERT DOCK, LIVERPOOL

Built between 1841 and 1848, this complex comprises a massive 7½ acres of enclosed water and 1.3 million sq ft of warehouse floor space. The Albert Dock, opened in July 1846 by the Prince Consort himself, was designed by dock engineer Jesse Hartley, a no-nonsense Yorkshireman renowned for his rough manner and colourful language. Hartley's buildings are fireproof, being made of brick, granite and iron, with no wood used in their construction except for the piling. Their uniform arrangement in a neat quadrangle, solidly perched on unfluted Greek Doric columns of hollow cast iron, forms

one of the noblest and most dignified architectural ensembles of the Victorian era. Once again, a humble engineer had shown how to do things properly. It is a measure of its true significance that a model of the Albert Dock was displayed at the Great Exhibition of 1851 and attracted considerable attention. As ever, not everyone was impressed. In his *Memorials of Liverpool* of 1875, J A Picton called the Albert Dock 'a hideous pile of naked brickwork'. Time has proved such critics wrong. This splendid Victorian creation is now the proud centrepiece of a rejuvenated Liverpool waterfront.

TIME OFF

Palace Pier in Brighton was a replacement of the famous Chain Pier, which was destroyed by a great storm in 1896.

If just a single object has to be selected that encapsulates the attitudes and social etiquette of the Victorian seaside, then it surely is the bathing machine. The principal purpose of these cumbersome conveyances, which bear a striking resemblance to potting sheds on wheels, was to transport female bathers a short distance from the shore into the sea, where they could discreetly slip into the briny, safely shielded from the prying eyes of young men equipped with telescopes. Queen Victoria herself was initiated into this seaside ritual on 30 July 1847, after which she wrote: 'Drove down to the beach with my maid and went into the bathing machine, where I undressed and bathed in the sea (for the first time in my life), a very nice bathing woman attending me. I thought it delightful until I put my head under the water, when I thought I should be stifled.'

Doubtless, other Victorian ladies of lesser rank found the experience equally alarming, but the seaside – now only a quick journey from many inland cities and towns – had caught the public imagination. In the early days, steamers brought the crowds of holiday trippers to places along the coast. Far more dramatic in impact, however, was the railway network, which transformed numerous small fishing hamlets into fully fledged seaside resorts. Here, next to the unbridled mysteries of the deep, Victorian fantasies could run wild in an entirely new environment, one in which the stiff social conventions of the day could be judiciously relaxed if not entirely suspended.

Britain's seaside resorts, stretching from Margate and Bournemouth in the south to Blackpool and Scarborough in the north, are visibly Victorian in architectural style to this day. Their essential features consist of stately promenades, exotic bandstands, floral terraces, elegant benches and long jetties, featuring fantasy architecture, jutting out boldly into the sea. The seaside piers that survive today are a pale shadow of the many glories that once adorned the coasts of Britain. But the combined factors of natural disasters and expensive maintenance have taken their toll over the years. Far more enduring are the grand hotels, which continue to do good business in these much-changed times. Scarborough's Grand Hotel, which was designed by Cuthbert Brodick, the architect of Leeds Town Hall, is perhaps the most imposing of all these establishments, looking every inch a cliff-top château haughtily surveying the shoreline below.

Victorian enterprise played a key role in the development of the seaside resort. Welsh miners, brought over to Ilfracombe in 1836, hewed a passage through the solid rock in order to open up access to the aptly named Tunnel Beaches. Ingenious transport systems were devised in Saltburn, Scarborough and Lynton-Lynmouth to convey holidaymakers down to the beach and back. Magnus Volk's Electric Overland and Submarine Railway of 1883 in Brighton was Britain's very first electric railway. Blackpool's South Promenade pioneered the electric tramway in 1885. The same resort constructed in 1894 what must surely rank as the most audacious leisure attraction of all, the Blackpool Tower, standing at just more than half the height of the Eiffel Tower in Paris, on which the steel structure was modelled.

Victorian tourism was not confined to the seaside alone. The romantic spirit of the age found much satisfaction in the wild landscapes of the north. Victoria's unbridled enthusiasm for the Scottish Highlands, described in a best-selling travel book by the Queen herself, caused many others to follow in her royal footsteps and explore the lochs and the glens. The joys of mass travel were brought within reach of millions through the enterprise of Thomas Cook. His first travel group of 5 July 1841 comprised 500 temperance supporters from Leicester to Loughborough. This proved to be the start of many excursions, both at home and abroad. In 1851 Joseph Paxton, architect of the Crystal Palace, asked Cook to bring visitors from Yorkshire and the Midlands to London for the Great Exhibition. The success of this initiative was phenomenal, with some 150,000 people taking advantage of Cook's offer.

Meanwhile, many towns and cities were developing leisure facilities of their own. Palatial theatres, concert halls and opera houses were opening everywhere. Much of London's West End bears a strong Victorian imprint. Provincial entertainment was no less impressive: Newcastle's Theatre Royal of 1837 and Tyne Theatre & Opera House of 1867 would grace any metropolis. Public houses also found their highest expression as outlandish gin-palaces with an excess of mahogany, cut glass, engraved mirrors, colourful ceramics and shining brass. London boasts many fine examples of these magnificent buildings, such as the Princess Louise in Holborn, but Liverpool's glorious trio, consisting of the Philharmonic, Vines and Crown, is a true connoisseur's delight.

London's Russell Hotel, a terracotta extravaganza by Charles Fitzroy Doll, built in 1898, was opened with panache on Derby Day, 1900.

There was an enormous investment in public parks, which became an important focus for leisure activities in urban areas. The honour of founding the country's first municipal park went to Birkenhead in 1847. Liverpool's Sefton Park of 1872 is another fine example. Jesmond Dene in Newcastle, which was originally created by the industrialist Sir William Armstrong, was later gifted to the city. Everywhere, existing parks were embellished with formal gardens and elegant statuary.

Along with outdoor leisure pursuits, the Victorian age also witnessed a veritable explosion in organized sport. Football, formerly an exclusive, public school affair, became a popular national pastime with a strong working-class following. In 1888 the Football League was founded in Manchester, where in the Pump House People's History Museum you can catch a rare glimpse of a Victorian football match – Blackburn Rovers playing West Bromwich Albion in 1898 – via a short film clip of shaking, ghostly quality.

The growing popularity of lawn tennis brought about a change in the life of Victorian youth. The game took over from croquet as an acceptable activity where young men and ladies might meet. It was still considered improper for a lady to show her ankles, so long white dresses, corsets and bustles remained *de rigueur*. At a garden party of 1887, Thomas Hardy observed: 'Young people . . . so madly devoted to lawn tennis that they set about it like day-labourers at the moment of their arrival.' Ten years earlier the first championships had been played on the lawns of the All England Club. The Wimbledon Lawn Tennis Museum tells the whole exciting story.

Meanwhile, the age-old pursuits of hunting, shooting and fishing remained as popular as ever with the landed gentry. One only has to see the game books in any Victorian country house to realize that, in this respect, time had stood still, in line with the nostalgic style of the architecture. The Prince of Wales, a regular guest at such places, must have taken advantage of the services of a good many of the almost 6,000 gamekeepers employed in England and Scotland during the 1880s. The Prince was also a keen racegoer. At Waddesdon Manor, a painting of Goodwood in 1886 shows the Prince of Wales, with his customary cigarette in his hand, surrounded by the great and the good of the nation – a canvas that perfectly expresses the leisured life of the Victorian upper classes.

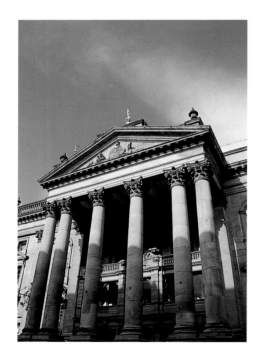

Built in 1837 and remodelled in 1901 by Frank Matcham, the Theatre Royal, Newcastle, neatly spans the entire Victorian era.

Osborne House on the Isle of Wight, a favourite holiday retreat for Victoria and Albert, permits some fascinating insights behind the scenes of the royal household. A statue of Victoria, which the young Queen had made in 1849 as a birthday present for her beloved Albert, greets visitors in the Grand Corridor. Poignant memories of the Prince Consort are everywhere. He appears in statue form in the guise of a noble Roman centurion or in a small portrait as a medieval knight in armour in the Queen's Bedroom where Victoria finally died on 22 January 1901. Her body lay in state in the Dining Room before being transported back to Windsor for burial. On a happier note, the exotic Victorian dream of India finds potent expression at Osborne House in the sumptuous Durbar Room where even the wealthiest maharajah might feel very much at home.

PHILHARMONIC HOTEL, LIVERPOOL

This most sophisticated late-Victorian public house designed by Walter Thomas between 1898 and 1900, has come through a century of existence remarkably unscathed. The Art Nouveau exterior presents a dazzling display of stepped gables, turrets, balconies and oriels, while the interior reveals a riot of decoration, the result of a fruitful collaboration between artists and craftsmen from the School of Architecture and Applied Art at Liverpool University. The lavish treatment extends through every detail of the bars right down to the luxury finish of the gentlemen's toilets, where marble and ceramics combine with porcelain to create a magnificent effect.

VINES, LIVERPOOL

In spite of dire warnings by the Temperance Movement about the evils of drink, Victorian publicans countered the negative associations of alcohol by creating some truly magnificent establishments of amazing luxury. Condemned as 'gin palaces', these ornate pubs remain the ultimate expression of their genre. The escalation of opulent materials and fanciful effect came to a climax around the turn of the century in such lavish productions as Liverpool's Vines, a heady concoction of mahogany, beaten copper and rich plasterwork . The carved caryatids still display their alluring feminine charms.

ITALIAN WATER GARDEN, HYDE PARK, LONDON

This noble creation at Victoria Gate brings the northern end of the contrived 'natural' curve of the Serpentine to a contrastingly formal conclusion. Laid out in 1861, the Italian Water Garden consists of an ensemble of fountains and basins set in a balustraded enclosure with classical ornamentation. The statuary by the lake, although noticeably eroded, conveys all the charm of a Renaissance garden. Other elements include an Italianate summer house and Queen Anne's Alcove, which was transferred from its original position in Kensington Gardens.

KIBBLE PALACE, GLASGOW

The new building technology of glass and iron displayed by Joseph Paxton at Chatsworth and, subsequently, in the Crystal Palace at the Great Exhibition of 1851 found numerous uses all over the country in covered structures, such as market halls and railway stations. But its original role for conservatories and greenhouses was not abandoned. Kibble Palace, in Glasgow's Botanic Gardens, was first built at Coulport on Loch Long in 1860. It was then re-erected in modified form on its present site in 1873. The central rotunda used to serve as a concert hall, but its interior is now a riot of ferns and palms. The marble statuary shows a typically Victorian brand of mild eroticism.

INCLINED TRAMWAY, SALTBURN

With the arrival of the Stockton & Darlington Railway in 1861, the seaside hamlet of Saltburn was poised for a dramatic transformation into a prestigious Victorian watering place. The splendid Zetland Hotel on the clifftop had its own platform at the back door, ready to receive guests arriving by rail. The resort has since fallen short of its lofty ambitions and remains curiously trapped in a pleasant time warp. As a result, Saltburn offers a most authentic Victorian seaside experience. The greatest attraction is the famous Inclined Tramway of 1884, which operates by water balance. The pier still exists, albeit in a shortened version following a storm in 1974, to provide a satisfying conclusion to what is surely one of the most exciting twenty seconds of public transport to be experienced anywhere in the country.

EASTBOURNE PIER

This stately structure of 1872 is a fine example of the Victorian seaside pier. These great jetties, extending far out into the sea, first evolved as landing stages for coastal steamers bringing visitors to the resorts. They rapidly became popular as somewhere to promenade and enjoy various sideshows, so that they soon developed into palaces of fun, offering gaudy attractions. Penny-in-the-slot machines tempted passers-by with a quick peep of forbidden fruits in 'What the Butler Saw', and suchlike. The risqué elements of the seaside resort offended stuffier souls. The Rev. Balmer wrote of his shocking experiences in 1899: 'I thought perhaps the pictures meant some beautiful representations of Paris, and dropped a penny in one of these abominable slots. It was like looking through a gateway to perdition.'

ST GEORGE'S HALL, LIVERPOOL

The foundation stone was laid on 28 June 1838 to mark the coronation of Queen Victoria, and few buildings express so perfectly the soaring ambitions of the age as St George's Hall in Liverpool. The original idea was for a concert hall to host the city's triennial music festivals. Harvey Lonsdale Elmes, a London architect, won the competition and proposed a plan for

a main hall accommodating 3,000 people and a concert room for 1,000. As an afterthought, it was decided to incorporate Liverpool's new Crown Court and Civil Court within the same structure. St George's Hall thus turned out to be a curious amalgam – an impressive cultural venue in the grand neo-classical manner but with a court of justice at either end of its magnificent Great Hall, and with police cells in the basement.

CRYSTAL PALACE, LONDON

After the astounding success of the Great Exhibition in 1851, visited by more than six million people from home and abroad, the glass-and-iron conservatory designed by Joseph Paxton was removed from Hyde Park to Sydenham in south London. Here, the Crystal Palace, as it now became known, was rebuilt and extended as a permanent attraction. The great edifice, divided into themed courts, hosted concerts, drama, exhibitions and menageries. There were fountains spouting water to a great height and regular displays of fireworks. The adjoining terrace gardens were adorned with exotic statuary. But for Ruskin, it had 'no more sublimity than a cucumber frame between two

chimneys'. Nevertheless, for more than eighty years the Crystal Palace pulled in the crowds until it went up in flames during the night of 30 November 1936. All that now remains is a handful of concrete sphinxes guarding the broad flights of steps leading up to the vacant site. The nearby amusement park is still going strong, and the ornamental lakes shelter a bizarre collection of prehistoric monsters of 1854 vintage, made of brick, iron and stucco. The greatest was the giant Iguanodon, which was so large that an inaugural dinner party for twenty-one scientists was held in its almost completed shell. Even today, as an empty space, the famous Crystal Palace exerts a strong fascination.

FAMILY HOLIDAYS, ISLE OF WIGHT

Osborne House provides a telling illustration of how Victoria and Albert liked to spend their leisure time. The royal couple bought the estate in 1845 and demolished the existing house. They then had a much grander one, designed by Thomas Cubitt in Albert's preferred Italianate style, erected in its place. At Osborne, the Prince Consort was in his element, even declaring that the Solent on a good day had similarities to the Bay of Naples. He took particular delight in designing the landscaped garden. In his characteristic way, Albert assumed total control of the proceedings. From the pavilion flag tower of Osborne House he directed by semaphore the planting of trees and ordered how the valley should be opened up, with the consequent

moving of vast quantities of earth. The restored terrace gardens reflect the Albertian effect of the previous century. Osborne served essentially as a place for long family holidays. At the Swiss Cottage the nine royal children could play to their hearts' content with such dream toys as a model Victoria Fort and Albert Barracks. The little princes and princesses were given a kitchen garden to manage, where Albert encouraged them to cultivate vegetables using scaled-down gardening tools. Victoria took up the new fashion of swimming in the sea, and her bathing machine has been preserved as a prize exhibit. This is a top-of-the-range model with its own plumbed-in WC. After Victoria's death, her luxury contraption was used for many years as a chicken shed.

VICTORIAN VIEWS OF SCOTLAND

The Queen's View at Loch Tummel and Scott's View of the Eildon Hills were two Scottish perspectives much admired by the royal couple. Especially in the Highlands they found a spiritual retreat away from the cares and stresses of modern life. Victoria became such a devotee of Scotland that, in 1867, she published her best-selling *Leaves from the Journal of our Life in the Highlands*. Grandiose scenery and the nobility of humble folk were the main attractions: 'This solitude, the romance and wild loveliness of everything here, the absence of hotels and beggars, the independent simple people, who all speak Gaelic here, all make beloved Scotland the proudest finest country in the world.' In line with the ideas of his time, Albert combined a love of nature with a passion for shooting anything in fur or feathers. While Albert stalked stags or took pot-shots at gannets, Victoria read from Sir Walter Scott or sketched. These pastimes made the Queen and Prince Consort the perfect prototypes for many other nineteenth-century travellers of a more ordinary sort who followed in their wake.

The rugged, romantic paintings by Landseer encapsulate the stirring qualities of the Scottish landscape that so enthralled Victoria and her contemporaries. Along with Osborne, Balmoral remained one of the Queen's favourite places.

KINLOCH CASTLE,
ISLE OF RUM

In 1891 Sir George Bullough inherited the Hebridean Isle of Rum from his father, a successful Lancashire industrialist. This was the heyday for wealthy folk to act out baronial fantasies in the wide-open spaces of Scotland, where vast tracts of depopulated land the size of English counties could be run as private sporting estates. Kinloch Castle, built by Bullough around the turn of the century as a splendid combination of residence and shooting lodge, supplies a perfect example of how the idea of Scotland pioneered by Victoria and Albert at Balmoral inspired countless imitators. Local legend has it that

Sir George paid the workmen, who were mainly from Lancashire, a daily supplement for wearing a kilt. Inside the castellated edifice of red Arran sandstone, a silent army of stags surveys the scene. A full-length portrait of Sir George Bullough, clad in kilt and sporran, looks down from the gallery. Lady Monica's leather-bound music scores lie on the grand piano as if she had just stepped outside and would be returning at any moment. Kinloch Castle is a genuine time capsule, and likely to remain so since the 1957 terms of sale of the Isle of Rum stipulated that house and contents should be kept unchanged in their original state.

DOING THE RIGHT THING

The Houses of Parliament helped to launch the Gothic Revival. The statue of Richard I, made by Marochetti in 1861, was praised by Ruskin.

In this age of glorious obsessions, where a difference of opinion could quickly become an issue of conflicting moral principles, architecture was no exception. The famous Battle of the Styles fought out between the supporters of Classical and Gothic soon went far beyond the realm of style for style's sake and took on all the passion of the great religious controversies of the day. As the debate evolved, so the Gothic lobby, who maintained that their style represented the true spirit of Christianity, denounced the Classicists as the new Pagans.

The scene was set for the Battle of the Styles by the Houses of Parliament, which had to be rebuilt after the fire of 1834. The new building, it was decided, should be Gothic in order to fit in with the surviving Westminster Hall and nearby Westminster Abbey. In this respect the choice of Charles Barry as architect, a noble exponent of Italianate, might seem unlikely. But Barry had the perfect collaborator in the person of the passionate medievalist Augustus Welby Northmore Pugin. It was Pugin's inspired decorative flourishes that gave us the stunning external and internal Gothic appearance and set the overall style of the building in a quintessentially Victorian fashion.

Pugin went on to devote himself to what he considered to be purer expressions of Gothic in cathedrals such as St Mary's in Newcastle and St Chad's in Birmingham. Pugin also elaborated in his various writings, such as *The True Principles of Pointed or Christian Architecture* of 1841, his personal philosophy of the true spirit of the Middle Ages. His theories were to inspire both Ruskin and Morris. According to Pugin, Gothic was the only acceptably Christian form of architecture, although this conveniently ignored the fact that Christianity was older than the pointed arch. Meanwhile, the question of style became ever more heated. Oxford witnessed some fiery exchanges. The new University Museum turned out to be resoundingly Gothic. The chemistry laboratory was actually a copy of the medieval Abbot's Kitchen at Glastonbury. One scandalized Oxford academic even denounced it as 'inappropriate to use Gothic for a secular purpose'.

The industrialist Sir Titus Salt founded these Victorian almshouses in his model factory village at Saltaire, Yorkshire.

Stylistic controversies aside, all Victorians agreed on the need to do worthy things. The serious-minded Prince Albert, with his Germanic respect for *Kultur*, struck a vibrant chord among his contemporaries. Albert's abiding legacy, built with the profits of the Great Exhibition of 1851, is the splendid complex of museums in South Kensington. Here, all rule-books of correct style are thrown to the winds in a delightful outpouring of eclectic whimsy, which is typically late Victorian. The work carried on long after Albert's premature death in 1861, and the area came to be known as Albertopolis in his memory.

Less elevated folk were also keen to leave their name on some worthy enterprise. Josephine and John Bowes spent their fortune amassing a phenomenal collection of art and furniture, for which they built a convincing imitation of a French château at Barnard Castle in Co. Durham in order to house it. Their aim was educational, in a very Victorian way – namely to bring the world of art into the lives of ordinary people. Sadly, neither of these public-spirited people lived to witness the completion of their magnificent project in 1892.

In 1859 Louisa, Marchioness of Waterford, inherited the estates of her husband Henry, 3rd Marquis of Waterford. These included the village of Ford in Northumberland, where Louisa settled down to a modest life promoting temperance and doing good works. In the village school at Ford, which she had personally endowed, she commenced her 'great experiment' in 1862 to decorate the walls of the schoolroom with edifying scenes from the Bible. Using local children and their parents as models, Louisa devoted all her energies to the project from 1862 to 1883, creating one of the most spectacular of artistic monuments in what is a wild and remote corner of the country.

Such grassroots philanthropic effort so far from the social limelight would not have appealed to Thomas Holloway. He once advertised for worthy ideas on which to spend his huge fortune. His lasting personal memorial and major achievement survives today as the Royal Holloway College at Egham in Surrey, which is now part of the University of London. Here, even the most blasé observer will be taken aback by the sheer scale and flamboyance of the fanciful building, which Holloway commissioned from William Crossland. Suffice it to say that it upstages the French château on which it is modelled.

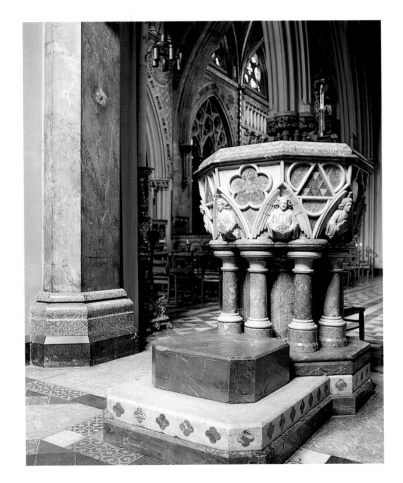

All Saints, Margaret Street, London, displays the polychrome effect promoted by the High Church Tractarian Movement.

The Buxton Memorial Fountain in Victoria Tower Gardens, London, commemorates a lesser known Victorian philanthropist. Sir Thomas Fowell Buxton, a successful brewer with a social conscience, was created a baronet by Queen Victoria. As befitting his role as leader of the Anti-Slavery Party, this monument marks the emancipation of slaves throughout the British Empire. The charming Gothic fountain, designed by SS Teulon in typically Victorian medievalist style, was originally erected in 1865 by Sir Thomas's son, Charles, in Parliament Square, and it was subsequently moved to its present location in 1957.

The refrain of education runs through the era as the worthiest of human endeavours. From élite establishments, such as Lancing College and Cheltenham Ladies College, down to publicly funded schools of the London School Board or the Church of England, the Victorians had a firm belief in decently run institutions, which could turn most human beings into useful members of society. There was a rash of new universities in the booming industrial towns. Alfred Waterhouse's design for Liverpool and George Gilbert Scott's for Glasgow rank among the most impressive. Gradually, women came to be regarded as more than breeders and rearers of children. Oxford and Cambridge acquired their first women's colleges, but the Royal Holloway College, which was opened in 1886, was the first institution to award university degrees to women.

For those who transgressed, the Victorian era was unforgiving. The noble Gothic of London's Royal Courts of Justice by G E Street might appear to offer spiritual solace of sorts, but prison architecture aimed to be a forbidding reminder of the consequences of crime. The grim interiors of Strangeways in Manchester or of Pentonville or Wormwood Scrubs in London proclaimed that atonement for crimes committed remained the essential ingredient in the penal medicine. As can be seen by the treadmill installed at Beaumaris Jail on Anglesey, the Victorians applied the notion of physical punishment very rigorously. And even in the Prison Chapel in Lincoln Castle, they took the principle of solitary confinement to its ultimate logical conclusion.

Victorian institutions, from schools and churches to hospitals, prisons and the workhouse, all seem imbued with the powerful idea that social problems could be solved by applying appropriate measures, and with relevant buildings to match. Although this unshakeable faith in society's capacity to improve the human condition may have turned out to be over optimistic, the Victorian passion for 'doing the right thing' was generally guided by the worthiest of motives, and many of the problems that were being addressed were relatively new phenomena born of the industrial and urban boom that was the hallmark of the age.

HOUSE OF LORDS, WESTMINSTER

This sumptuous interior, by Augustus Welby Northmore Pugin, ranks as a lofty pinnacle of Victorian Gothic. For this *tour de force* Pugin produced as many as 2,000 drawings detailing every aspect of the House of Lords. Pugin's creativity also had a practical side. His designs for everything, from furniture and wallpaper down to inkwells and umbrella stands, took into account not only the forms of medieval art but also the technical demands of modern manufacture. The canopy of the Sovereign's Throne is a real masterpiece, alive with miniature statues of medieval knights in armour. Curiously, Pugin himself was rather dismissive of the overall result at Westminster: 'All Grecian,

sir; Tudor details on a Classic body.' In truth, Pugin had to work his Gothic designs around the Classical plans drawn up by the architect Barry. But Pugin's House of Lords stands out, nevertheless, as a great shrine of Victorian Gothic. Its lavish medievalism was taken up all over the country, and it remains Pugin's most significant commission, which best displays his perfectionism and passionate commitment to reviving the very spirit of the Middle Ages. It is hard to believe that Pugin was in his early twenties at the time. He was only forty when he died, sadly insane, in 1852. But Pugin had lived long enough to see through his design for the Medieval Court at the Great Exhibition, a building that he disdainfully called 'the greenhouse'.

ROYAL ALBERT HALL, LONDON

With the profits of the Great Exhibition, Prince Albert proposed that a large piece of South Kensington should be purchased for building cultural institutions, such as museums, colleges and libraries. But the preliminary plans for a large concert hall had to be shelved, and the great project could not be realized until well after Albert's death in 1861. Captain Francis Fowke of the Royal Engineers drew up the architectural plans, and in 1868 Queen Victoria laid the foundation stone, declaring that the words 'Royal Albert' were to be added to the proposed name of 'Hall of Arts and Sciences'. The Albert Hall, as it is now generally known, is a worthy Victorian achievement, which still occupies a unique place in the cultural life of the country.

NATURAL HISTORY MUSEUM, LONDON

Another enduring monument to Prince Albert's cultural investment in Albertopolis was the Natural History Museum, opened in 1881. The striking design by Alfred Waterhouse is not in his usual red-blooded Gothic but a paler German Romanesque. The building is entirely fronted with honey-brown and grey-blue terracotta tiles and adorned with statues of beasts, both living and extinct. A statue of Adam used to occupy a pedestal on the gable above the main entrance – for some reason there was no room for Eve – but this image of the superior being in God's creation disappeared mysteriously during the last war. In this respect, the Natural History Museum seems to reflect the Victorian quandary of reconciling Darwinian theories of evolution with religious notions of the divine origin of human life.

KEBLE COLLEGE CHAPEL, OXFORD

This remarkable building represents the spiritual essence of the college, founded in 1868 in memory of John Keble (1792–1866) and paid for by public subscription. Keble had been a leader of the Oxford Movement, which campaigned for an Anglican return to certain 'Catholic' pre-Reformation doctrines and opposed the involvement of the State in the Church of England. Keble College, designed by William Butterfield, announced its arrival on the Oxford scene with a bold flourish of red brick. Even while the Oxford Movement was still going strong, the Warden of Keble, Edward Talbot, shook off the college's narrow ecclesiastical mission and widened its intellectual scope. But it remains an impressive monument to a very significant Victorian idea. Holman Hunt's painting *The Light of the World* hangs in the Chapel.

UNIVERSITY MUSEUM, OXFORD

It was resolved in 1849 to construct a building in Oxford that would assemble 'the materials explanatory of the organic beings placed upon the globe'. There was some resistance at the time to the teaching of science at Oxford University, and one of the first events in the new building, which was completed in 1860, was the momentous gathering of the British Association, at which Samuel Wilberforce, Bishop of Oxford, attacked Professor Thomas Huxley over the latter's support for the Darwinian theory of evolution. Ruskin's ideas are thought to have influenced Benjamin Woodward's Gothic Revival for the University Museum, a style that Tennyson considered 'perfectly indecent'. In true Victorian fashion, the controversy about the building was as passionate as that surrounding the theories of Darwin.

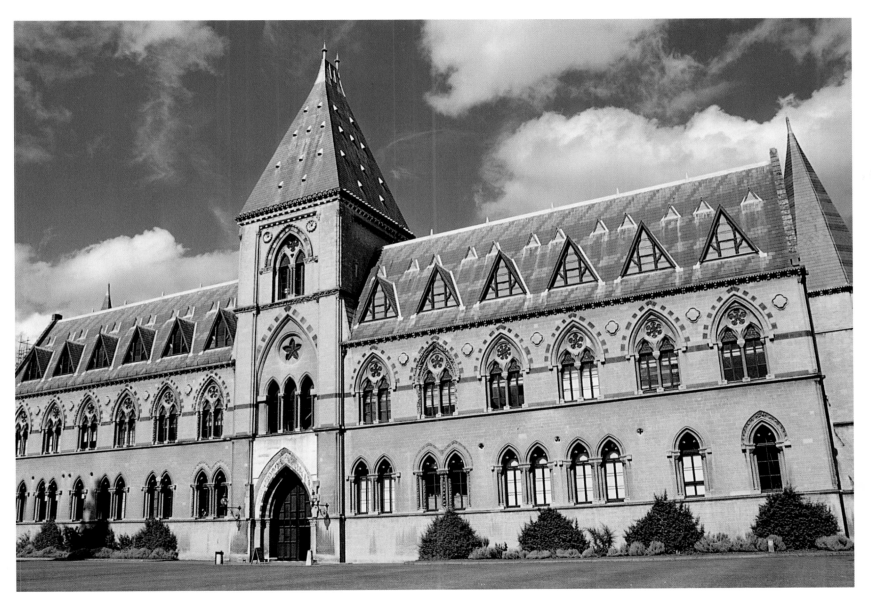

JOHN RYLANDS LIBRARY, MANCHESTER

When the Manchester millionaire John Rylands died in 1888, leaving a fortune of £2,750,000, his third wife and widow, Enriqueta Augustina Rylands, decided that building a public library in his native city was the right thing to do with her massive inheritance. She commissioned Basil Champneys, architect of Mansfield College, Oxford, to design a noble edifice, which would put Manchester on the map as home to one of the finest libraries in the land. The John Rylands Library has since been acclaimed as one of the greatest works of the Gothic Revival. This impressive act of remembrance also succeeded in its academic purpose, since it is now a valuable research facility as part of the Manchester University Library, with which it merged in 1972.

MANSFIELD COLLEGE, OXFORD

With High Church interests spectacularly catered for by Keble College, the Nonconformists of the Free Churches eventually gained a foothold in Oxford with the building in 1887–89 of Mansfield College. In contrast to Keble, Mansfield did not attempt to upstage the traditional colleges with a new style of architecture. Basil Champneys elected for a modest Gothic Revival that was very much in tune with Oxford University's medieval roots. The Chapel contains some beautiful Victorian stained glass as well as several sober statues of Reformist heroes, such as Luther, Calvin, Knox and Wycliffe. The Dining Hall and Library display some lovely decorative touches that are most evocative of the period.

THE NOBLE WORKS OF THOMAS HOLLOWAY

Thomas Holloway (1800–83) made a huge fortune with his pills and potions and bold international investments. Holloway then decided to dedicate his boundless energies to spending his wealth in lavish style on worthy works. His first project, from 1871, was a sanatorium in Virginia Water to cure the mental afflictions of the middle classes not rich enough to afford private treatment, nor poor enough to be cared for by public charity. The eye-dazzling decor of demented beasts chasing and attacking each other was the bizarre inspiration of William Crossland, architect of Rochdale Town Hall. Even before that project was completed, the two men had started on the

building of a college at nearby Egham, where women might develop their true potential through a proper university-style education. This was a progressive notion for Victorian Britain, and Holloway was determined to trumpet his intentions with a bombastic display of architecture modelled on the Château de Chambord. Queen Victoria opened the magnificent complex on 30 June 1886, some three years after the benefactor's death. But Thomas Holloway had already ensured a lasting presence for himself with numerous references to his munificence stuck up all over the buildings, as well as a prominent statue of himself as the great philanthropist indicating with outstretched hand to his wife Jane all the wonders he had created.

ROYAL COURTS OF JUSTICE, LONDON

In 1865 an expanse of land to the north of the Strand was purchased and one of London's foul Victorian slums demolished to make way for a public building of great importance. Designed by George Edmund Street, the Law Courts – as they are generally known – brought a touch of ecclesiastical style to a secular purpose. This is readily apparent inside, with the long vault of the Great Hall, which assumes the proportions of a small cathedral. The Law Courts marked the zenith of the Gothic Revival, all eleven designs submitted in the 1860s being in that style. In the years following their opening in 1882, Gothic was no longer dominant but simply one of many historical styles that architects picked and mixed with gay abandon.

PRISON CHAPEL, LINCOLN CASTLE

A model institution in its day, the prison block of 1845 inside Lincoln Castle made a speciality of solitary confinement under the new Pentonville or Separation System. Prisoners even wore special hoods during communal exercise to prevent any eye contact with their fellow inmates. The strict regime was also maintained during the obligatory chapel services. An ingenious arrangement of high-sided pews arranged as single cells permitted the inmates a view of the preacher in his pulpit, but of nobody else. The ruthless efficiency of Lincoln's state-of-the-art Separation System caused many a nervous breakdown and eventually had to be scrapped. The prison chapel, the only surviving original example of its kind, remains today as a chilling reminder of a failed social experiment.

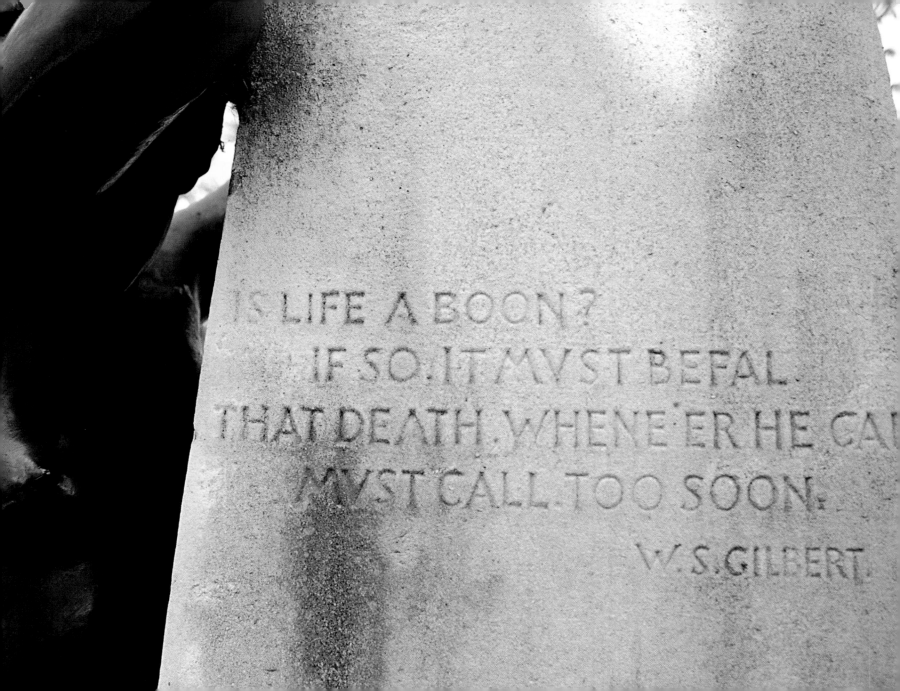

In Memoriam

The Sullivan Monument in Victoria Embankment Gardens, London, expresses a poignant reflection on mortality.

'Who is not made better and wiser by occasional intercourse with the tomb?' This very Victorian question posed in a very Victorian way appeared in George Blair's *Biographic and Descriptive Sketches of the Glasgow Necropolis* of 1857. This stately burial ground for better-off Glaswegians was laid out in the 1830s as a veritable city of the dead. In 1849, during a visit to Glasgow Cathedral, Prince Albert looked across to the nearby hillside bristling with funerary monuments and expressed himself delighted with the noble prospect.

The Glasgow Necropolis was typical of the new style of metropolitan cemetery making an appearance in major Victorian cities. According to its promoters, this 'much wanted accommodation for the higher classes' aimed to be 'respectful to the dead, safe and sanitary to the living, dedicated to the Genius of Memory and to extend religious and moral feeling'. It was indeed soon proving so popular with the living that it ranked as one of the city's leading tourist attractions. In the course of the month of July 1878 as many as 13,733 people were counted visiting the Glasgow Necropolis.

The vogue for constructing grand cemeteries allowed prosperous Victorians to give expression to their belief in an afterlife commensurate with the social station that they had so painstakingly achieved in this, the physical world. These burial grounds were laid out like garden suburbs with avenues winding scenically beneath the trees. The choicest grave sites were snapped up as eagerly as if they were house plots in a newly fashionable area. Some tombs resembled miniature temples, freely drawing inspiration from Byzantium, Rome, Greece and Egypt as well as from the Gothic of the Middle Ages.

However, even with their magnificent funereal architecture – as witnessed in London's Highgate, Brompton, West Norwood and Kensal Green cemeteries – the Victorians were far from reconciled to the mortality of all flesh. The composer Sir Arthur Sullivan's monument in Victoria Embankment Gardens has a tragic muse leaning in despair on his obelisk, which bears a wistful inscription by W S Gilbert reflecting that the visit of the Grim Reaper will always be too early for those on whom he calls.

In an age that saw no limits to human progress, death was perceived, inevitably, as the villain of the piece, striking down not only the weak and the aged but also claiming its unsuspecting victims at random among the young and the healthy. Victorian cemeteries are full of weeping angels to express the acute grief of premature bereavement or truncated

Not all Victorian cemeteries were in the grand manner. The small churchyard of St Mary Magdalen in Mortlake, one of the few Roman Catholic burial grounds in the London area at the time, was a modest affair compared with Highgate or Brompton.
Now delightfully overgrown and overshadowed by mature trees, the churchyard exudes a sweet, wistful atmosphere of times past. Many of the monuments are of a typically Victorian character with their elegiac inscriptions and charming statues of angels praying for the souls of the deceased.

Glasgow Necropolis was one of the new cemeteries built on a lavish scale to provide an appropriately impressive setting for the graves of prosperous Victorians. Nothing could be more public than this open hilltop looking across to Glasgow Cathedral. Crowning the summit, a statue of John Knox keeps a watchful eye on an eclectic collection of tombs clustered around the base of his lofty column.
The amenities of the Glasgow Necropolis were also enjoyed by living Glaswegians, who thereby acquired a valuable park ideal for a gentle stroll.

columns to symbolize the sudden snapping of a human life. As for the poor, if they were lucky, their names might be carved on the simple headstone of a communal Guinea Grave, such as may still be seen in Becket Street Cemetery in Leeds.

Commemoration of the dearly departed absorbed considerable energy and assumed a wide variety of forms. Quirkiness abounds in individual monuments. An upturned boat tops the tomb in Brompton Cemetery of Robert Coombes, 'champion sculler of the Thames and Tyne', who died in 1860. The Greek Doric monument to the 1st Earl of Durham on Penshaw Hill, in Co. Durham, is a half-sized copy of the Theseum in Athens. At Otley, in Yorkshire, a miniature castellated tunnel entrance adorns the graves of the railwaymen who died constructing the original. Nelson's Column in London's Trafalgar Square is a Victorian memorial to a Georgian hero, and it was completed in 1843 – although Landseer's famous lions, which adorn its base, did not make their appearance until almost a quarter of a century later, in 1867. Meanwhile, in 1852, the Duke of Wellington finally earned himself a prestigious neo-classical monument in St Paul's Cathedral.

When it came to commemorating an emperor, something special was called for. The death of Napoleon III of France at his Chislehurst exile in 1873 left Empress Eugénie with a son for consolation. But Louis, Napoleon's son, died a soldier's death fighting the Zulus in 1879. After this second tragedy, Eugénie resolved to build a suitable memorial to house the tombs of her husband and child. Saint Michael's Abbey, Farnborough, in Hampshire, which was completed between 1883 and 1888, was the result. French architect Gabriel Destailleur designed the buildings, which still shelter a Benedictine community. The bodies of the Emperor, Empress and the Prince Imperial lie in granite coffins in the crypt.

After the death of Albert in 1861, Victoria channelled her grief into constructing the Royal Mausoleum at Frogmore near Windsor. Work on the building, designed in the Prince Consort's favourite style of thirteenth-century Italy, lasted almost ten years, with the internal decoration being completed in August 1871. Here the widowed Queen would often come for spiritual comfort and contemplate her final resting-place at her husband's side. The mausoleum entrance is guarded by two winged, bronze angels, added in

1878, one bearing a trumpet and the other wielding a sword. The Royal Mausoleum is open to the public on only seven days a year, when it is possible to see the splendid white marble effigies of Victoria and Albert created by Baron Carlo Marochetti.

Victoria's personal grief found expression in a series of poignant private gestures. The Blue Room at Windsor, where Albert died on 13 December 1861, was left untouched. His gloves, cane and hat were laid out as if he might still need them. Hot water was brought every single evening during the remainder of the Queen's lifetime. A marble bust was set up on a column next to the bed where he died. Victoria was a regular visitor to the death chamber: 'When in an agony of loneliness, grief and despair, I kneel by that bed where He left us, decked with flowers and pray earnestly to be enabled to be courageous, patient and calm, and to be guided by my darling to do what He would wish; then a calm seems to come over me, a certainty my anguish is seen and heard not in vain, and I feel lifted above this miserable earth of sorrows.'

In addition to building the Royal Mausoleum at Frogmore, where Albert was laid to his final rest, Victoria had part of St George's Chapel in Windsor Castle converted into the Albert Memorial Chapel. Here, in a niche at the foot of the Prince Consort's symbolic tombchest, is a small statue of poignant emotion showing his widow distraught and weeping. The Victoria Memorial, located outside Buckingham Palace and dedicated to the glorious memory of the Queen herself, is a more grandiose posthumous production, and was erected by her son Edward VII.

By contrast, nothing could be more modest than the rustic grave of William Morris, shared with his wife and daughters, in the churchyard of St George, Kelmscott, where he was laid to rest on a wet and windy October day in 1896. A little wagon served as a hearse. The coffin lay on a bed of moss and willow branches. The funeral was heart breaking in its simplicity, according to Edward Burne-Jones, who described the loss of his dear friend in the most moving terms: 'The king was being buried and there were no others left.' To the adherents of the Arts and Crafts Movement and of the many other causes Morris espoused, that may serve as an epitaph to the Victorian age as a whole.

Jesmond Old Cemetery is an attractive and dignified last resting place for the citizens of Newcastle.

HIGHGATE CEMETERY, LONDON

The Bishop of London consecrated London's most prestigious Victorian cemetery in 1839. It soon became a fashionable place to be buried. In this city of the dead, the best grave monuments congregate in the most agreeable spots, suggesting a form of social segregation as rigorous as in the city of the living. The tomb architecture echoes the prevailing 'Battle of the Styles' with Gothic and Greek leading the field, followed by Egyptian and Byzantine. The serpentine paths lead to enchanting vistas and even to scaled-down replicas of urban forms, such as the circus. The Circle of Lebanon, with its noble array of front doors, remains one of the best addresses in Highgate Cemetery. The venture proved so popular that an extension was opened in 1857.

BROMPTON CEMETERY, LONDON

The land was acquired in 1837 and consecrated in 1840. According to the initial plans, this was to be as an ambitious undertaking, with a broad central avenue leading to an octagonal chapel with an imposing dome. In addition to this Anglican chapel, there were to have been separate ones for Catholics and Nonconformists, but financial problems intervened and they were never built. Likewise, the Great Circle of catacombs could not be completed, although the bold layout of the scheme can be readily appreciated. Brompton's close proximity to Kensington may be the reason why eminent persons such as Francis Fowke, architect of the Royal Albert Hall, and Henry Cole, organizer of the Great Exhibition, are buried here.

SCOTT MONUMENT, EDINBURGH

The towering spire built in Edinburgh in 1844 to commemorate the romantic poet and novelist Sir Walter Scott enjoyed a mixed reception at the time. It was immediately condemned by some as an alien Gothic monstrosity marring the noble prospect of Edinburgh's neo-classical New Town. The winner of the architectural competition was an unknown country joiner called George Meikle Kemp. This commission turned out to be his one and only, since he drowned in the Union Canal before work had been completed. Critical opinions of the monument have since mellowed. The Scott Monument has become a popular and distinctive Edinburgh landmark on Princes Street. It prefigures by more than twenty years some of the features of the Albert Memorial.

GUARDS' CRIMEAN MONUMENT, LONDON

This memorial in Waterloo Place, London, is partly made from Russian cannon captured at Sebastopol in 1855. Designed by John Bell in 1860, it is crowned by a traditional figure of Victory, but the main feature is the sombre group of guards in greatcoats and bearskins. This commemoration of the 2,162 officers, NCOs and men of the three regiments of foot guards who lost their lives during the Crimean War pioneered the idea of building war memorials to the dead. One of the outcomes of the Crimean military fiasco, which shook Victorian self-belief to its foundations, was the heroic work of Florence Nightingale, who brought to national attention the need for proper medical units in the armed services. Fittingly, her statue stands nearby.

PYRAMID TOMB, LIVERPOOL

Wit makes an occasional appearance in the serious business of grave design. This pyramid-shaped tomb in Liverpool contains the mortal remains of William Mackenzie, who died in 1851. According to the last wishes of the deceased, a compulsive card player, his body was entombed in a seated position, and he holds forever, clasped in his hand, a winning ace. The Egyptian pyramid, one of the most ancient forms of funerary architecture, was particularly popular among those Victorians in search of something more exotic than home-grown Gothic or the more usual Greek and Roman revivals in order to provide a direct and powerful symbol of their hopes for eternity.

BURTON TOMB, MORTLAKE, LONDON

Individual eccentricity is perfectly expressed in the tomb of the intrepid explorer Sir Richard Burton (1821–90) and his wife, Lady Isabel, in the churchyard of St Mary Magdalen. The monument, in the form of an Arabian tent, is adorned with stars and crescents as well a crucifix. Burton, whose achievements as an adventurous traveller in Africa, South America and the Middle East were partly overshadowed by his racy translation of the Arabian Nights, had wished to be buried together with his wife in a real Bedouin tent. Lady Isabel did the best she could with this concrete replica and she joined her husband here when she died on 22 March 1896. Their separate coffins can be viewed through a skylight at the rear.

THE WATTS CHAPEL

The Watts Memorial Chapel of 1898 at Compton in Surrey took funerary art into a higher realm. This small Byzantine chapel covered with terracotta sculpture was the creation of Mary Seton Watts, wife of the successful painter George Frederic Watts.

The exquisite interior seethes with Art Nouveau symbolism and Celtic mysticism. Mary Watts, who was an accomplished artist in her own right, sought advice from a galaxy

of famous Victorian painters. In order to complete the Watts Chapel she also enlisted the help of the village community in whose cemetery it stands. Exceptionally, for a Victorian monument commemorating death, the Compton Chapel celebrates the eternally mysterious forces of life. It brings a new spiritual dimension of hope and acceptance to the prevailing mood of gloom and despair. George Frederic and Mary Seton Watts are buried nearby.

ALBERT MEMORIAL, LONDON

In 1862, the year after the death of Prince Albert, the Lord Mayor of London launched a fund-raising campaign to erect a fitting memorial. A committee examined the submissions, but the Queen herself selected the winning design, by George Gilbert Scott. Public subscriptions were augmented by the exceptional sum of £50,000 voted by Parliament. By 1872, the Albert Memorial was complete, except for the statue of the Prince, which was installed in 1876. Four sculptural groups symbolize the continents of Europe, Asia, Africa and America. Allegorical figures of Engineering, Manufactures, Agriculture and Commerce sum up

the practical achievements of the nineteenth century. Albert's cultural interests feature in the Parnassus Frieze and in the glittering mosaics with their representations of Poetry, Painting and Sculpture. The sciences, including Geometry, Astronomy, Chemistry and Medicine, feature as symbolic statues. Altogether, the Albert Memorial amounts to a comprehensive celebration of a remarkable age. Having braved long years of neglect, and even the threat of demolition, the Albert Memorial has at last been sensitively restored by English Heritage so that this most potent expression of High Victorian civilization can be appreciated by future generations.

A maiden pours water in an endless stream from a pitcher in the Italian Water Garden, Hyde Park, London.

BIBLIOGRAPHY

Archer, John H G, *Art and Architecture in Victorian Manchester*, Manchester University Press, 1985

Ayris, Ian, *A City of Palaces – Richard Grainger and the Making of Newcastle upon Tyne*, Newcastle Libraries & Arts, 1997

Best, Geoffrey, *Mid-Victorian Britain 1851–75*, Weidenfeld & Nicolson, 1971 (and Fontana, 1979)

Briggs, Asa, *Victorian Cities*, Odhams Press, 1963 (and Penguin, 1990)

Briggs, Asa, *Victorian People*, Odhams Press, 1954 (and Penguin, 1990)

Briggs, Asa, *Victorian Things*, Batsford 1988 (and Penguin, 1990)

Clark, Kenneth, *The Gothic Revival*, John Murray, 1962

Curl, James Stevens, *Victorian Architecture*, David & Charles, 1990

Dixon, Roger and Muthesius, Stefan, *Victorian Architecture*, Thames & Hudson, 1978

Elliott, John, *Palaces, Patronage & Pills – Thomas Holloway: His Sanatorium, College & Picture Gallery*, Royal Holloway, University of London, 1996

Girouard, Mark, *The Victorian Country House*, Yale University Press, 1979

Girouard, Mark, *Victorian Pubs*, Studio Vista, 1975

Girouard, Mark, *Sweetness and Light – the Queen Anne Movement 1860–1900*, Clarendon Press, 1977

Harrison, J F C, *The Early Victorians 1832–51*, Weidenfeld & Nicolson 1971 (republished as *Early Victorian Britain 1832–51*, Fontana, 1979)

Harrison, J F C, *Late Victorian Britain 1875–1901*, Routledge, 1991

Lambton, Lucinda, *Vanishing Victoriana*, Elsevier Phaidon, 1976

Le Quesne, A L [et al], *Victorian Thinkers (Carlyle, Ruskin, Arnold, Morris)*, Oxford University Press, 1993

Newsome, David, *The Victorian World Picture*, John Murray, 1997

Orbach, Julian, *Victorian Architecture in Britain* (Blue Guide), A & C Black, 1987

Simmons, Jack, *The Victorian Railway*, Thames & Hudson, 1991

Victoria, Queen of Great Britain, *Leaves from the Journal of our Life in the Highlands 1848–1861*, London, 1868

Victoria, Queen of Great Britain, *More Leaves from the Journal of a Life in the Highlands 1862–1882*, London, 1884

ACKNOWLEDGEMENTS

In writing this book I am indebted to many people. Particular thanks for invaluable help with travel arrangements are due to Val Lowther of the Northumbria Tourist Board; Lis Phelan, Marie Mohan and Helen Hipkiss of Marketing Manchester, Graham Fish of Greater Manchester Districts Tourism Forum, Joe McConnell of the Birmingham Marketing Partnership, Neil Rami and Debra Westlake of The Mersey Partnership. I am grateful to the following for showing me the Victorian sights of their cities: Simon Brooks in Newcastle, Hilary Oxlade in Liverpool, Lynne Maud and Ian Stubbs in Middlesbrough, Jonathan Schofield in Manchester, Dennis Wellar in Saltburn and John Elliot, for his introduction to Thomas Holloway at Egham and Virginia Water.

I would also like to thank the following for their practical assistance in the course of my researches and photography: Arundel Castle, Beamish North of England Open Air Museum, Birkenhead Tramways, Black Country Museum, Brantwood, Buckingham Palace, Cardiff Castle, Castell Coch, Chetham's Library, Compton Parish Council, Darlington Railway Centre & Museum, Didcot Railway Centre, Discovery Museum in Newcastle, English Heritage, Foreign & Commonwealth Office (David Grieve), Glasgow City Council, Highclere Castle (the Earl of Carnarvon), Highgate Cemetery, HMS *Warrior*, House of Commons, House of Lords, Isle of Wight Steam Railway, John Rylands Library, Josephine & John Bowes Museum, Keble College, Kelmscott Manor, Kinloch Castle, Leighton House, Lincoln Castle, Mansfield College, The Maritime Trust, Middlesbrough Borough Council, Morwellham Quay Museum, Museum of Science & Industry in Manchester, Museum of Welsh Life St Fagan's, National Museums & Galleries on Merseyside, National Railway Museum, National Trust, National Trust for Scotland, National Waterways Museum, Octagon Developments Ltd, The Philharmonic in Liverpool, Pumphouse People's History Museum in Manchester, Red House Bexleyheath, Rochdale Metropolitan Borough Council, Rochdale Pioneers Museum, Royal Courts of Justice, Royal Holloway & Bedford New College, St George's Hall Liverpool, St Michael's Abbey in Farnborough, Sherlock Holmes Museum, SS *Great Britain*, Swindon Railway Heritage Centre Trust, Thomas Cook Archives, Torbay Borough Council, Victoria & Albert Museum, The Victorian Society, The Watts Gallery, Vines in Liverpool, Wheal Martyn Museum, Wigan Pier, Wimbledon Lawn Tennis Museum, Windsor Castle, Woodchester Mansion Trust, Wookey Hole Mill.

INDEX